A History of Leadville, Colorado

Marshall Conant Graff

Appears to have been written in 1915 or 1916. VM

TABLE OF CONTENTS

LEADVILLE, COLORADO

CHAPTER I

THE PLACER PERIOD

The Indians in Mexico told the early Spanish invaders fabulous stories of great villages and wonderful gold mines far to north. The "great villages" were undoubtedly the Pueblo villages to the south while probably, the "wonderful gold mines" were the placer mines of this very region. These stories induced Coronado in 1540 to lead a company of 800 Spaniards and Mexicans northward in search of gold. These were the first white men in Colorado.[1]

The region of the Arkansas Valley was at one time claimed by France as a part of Louisiana and also claimed by Spain as a part of Mexico. The eastern half of the state of Colorado became part of the United States by the Louisiana purchase of 1803, and the western half by the treaty of Guadalupe Hidalgo in 1848, Leadville being just about upon the line between the acquisitions. After the Louisiana purchase the United States Government sent out an expedition of twenty-three men of the regular army under the leadership of Lieutenant Pike, which reached the western Arkansas in October 1806, and came within sight of the Rocky Mountains November 15, of that year, when the most prominent peak was named after the commander. After passing a winter of

[1] Some authorities contend that Coronado's route did not take him through Colorado.

great severity in the mountains and discovering the rivers of Colorado, Pike and his comrades were taken prisoners by the Spaniards who had a military post in the San Louis Park or San Juan county. In 1819, a second expedition was sent to these mountains by the government. This was commanded by Colonel S. H. Long of the regular army. He followed the South Platte westward, named Long's Peak and carefully explored the country. In 1832 the American Fur Company also sent out an expedition under Captain Bonniville. But the most satisfactory expeditions were those sent out by the government under Freemont in 1842 and 1844.[1]

The earliest exploration of the Arkansas Valley was by Freemont in 1845. In his previous expeditions he had aimed at tracing the Arkansas river to its source, but unwittingly he had left the main stream, following up Fountain Creek and probably passed near the present site of Denver, but in 1845 he entered the mountains, where Canon City now stands and crossed the southern end of the South Park reaching the upper Arkansas Valley through that of Trout Creek, thence up the Arkansas and down the Eagle; this would indicate that the name of Freemont Pass would better have been given to Tennessee Pass, which divides the Arkansas and the Eagle, rather than that of Ten Mile Creek.[2] General Freemont left excellent maps showing Twin Lakes, Half Moon Creek, Lake Fork, etc. He also reports finding many elk, deer, antelope, and mountain sheep in this region.[3]

....

1 Fossett, Frank, Colorado (Edition of '76, Pp.10-13)

2 Emmons, S. F., Monograph on Leadville, P. 7.

3 Excellent accounts of Pike's, Long's, and Freemont's expedition is contained in Eugene Parson's "The Making of Colorado".

A few years later gold was discovered in California and thousands of weary travellers plodded and poured through Colorado little dreaming of the great riches so close at hand. At this time only a few Indians and fur traders occupied the plains. A trading post was established at Pueblo, but this was wiped out by the Ute Indians in 1854. Undoubtedly the Arkansas Valley was visited by trappers and individual explorers, but no records exist and the region was debatable territory between the Utes and the Arapohoes, both of whom used the region solely as a hunting ground, never making any permanent settlement.[1]

A trapper named Williams claims to have in 1848 penetrated into the South Park and to have discovered gold. During the year 1856 a party of Texas rangers entered the South Park via the Arkansas River. They skirted along the Mosquito range and camped nearly opposite the present site of Fairplay. Early in 1858 W. Green Russel and nine companions left Georgia for the purpose of searching for gold along the eastern slopes of the Rocky Mountains. This party prospected on nearly all the streams of northern Colorado, but returned disheartened in December to the Platte, where they camped at Dry Creek, and took therefrom several hundred dollars in gold dust. The news was brought back to the states by some of the party. The tidings spread like "wild fire". The panic of 1857 had thrown thousands out of employment and these were elated by the opportunity offered by the discovery of gold in Colorado.[2]

....

1 Emmons, P. 8
2 Fossett, 13-14.

In the winter wonderful stories regarding the Pike's Peak gold region (for this name had been applied to the entire country after the peak that first greeted the eye of the immigrant although no gold was found within fifty miles of it) were circulated throughout the states. The result as soon as spring opened was a grand stampede for the new Eldorado. Thousands streamed across the plains in an unbroken and apparently never ending procession of humanity and white-topped wagons, moving it seemed at a snails pace yet many bearing the legends, "Lightening Express", "Root Hog or Die", "From Pike County to Pike's Peak", and etc. The magic word "gold" had created a fever and enthusiasm that no distance or hardship could repress, no danger or difficulty dispell. The multitude swarmed and crept across the plains, some in wagons with ox teams, some on horseback and some on foot, all weary and footsore. Some carried their packs, others used pushcarts and one man had a wheelbarrow and took a boarder to help pay expenses. But all headed onward and westward to the land of promise. It is estimated that over 50,000 people came that year. All classes contributed to swell the human tide rushing for the gold fields. However,ninety-five per cent of them had absolutely no knowledge of gold-mining and had but little idea of the sufferings and hardships to be endured. Thousands arriving in Denver and finding no gold returned to civilization disgusted. Denver was the point of arrival and departure for nearly all who came or left the country. It was a second Babel. The arrival of teams, the shouting and the building,all contributed to the confusion, but nevertheless shanties and business

blocks arose with rapidity. Among the business houses established were three banks one of which, it is said, charged from 10% to 20% interest monthly on loans.[1]

The bones of men and mules marked the pathway to the West and the spirit was that of the slogan "Pike's Peak or bust", but the story of the deserted wagon bearing the legend "Busted by Gosh" describes the fate of many. A small town was started on Clear Creek; gold was discovered on Ralston's Creek and the Deadwood Diggings on South Boulder Creek payed well. The first gulch gold was taken out of Chicago Creek, although the Gregory diggings were started about the same time. These were discovered by John H. Gregory and Wilkes de Frees and proved a rich find and added greatly to the excitement and the stampede. Gregory took out $972 in one week and other rich strikes were made almost daily.[2]

Late in the fall of 1859 a party located gold in California Gulch, but it was too late to work their discovery; hence they agreed to keep their find a secret and return early the following spring. However the story leaked out and the original discoverers were "beaten in" the following spring by a group of prospectors, among whom S. S. Slater, George Stevers, Johh Currier, Abe Lee, Ike Rafferty, Tom Williams, and Dick Wilson were the leaders. The first hole dug in the gulch was about 200 feet above the present site of the Jorden tunnel, the second just above Oro.

....

[1] Fossett, 19-20

[2] Fossett, 20-23, and Alice P. Hill Tales of the Colorado Pioneers, P. 24. There is an interesting description of the Rush and the Growth of Denver in Parson's.

Gold was discovered in many places, as indicated by the fact that fourteen discovery claims were located.[1] There is a pretty story, although probably not true, that when these prospectors, who arrived in the spring of 1860 and who had obtained their information from the original discoverers, had crossed the great South Park and had found themselves in the valley of the Arkansas, Abe Lee, the head of one of these parties and William Jones, who headed the other, agreed that one party should go north into what is now Colorado Gulch, while the other would take the one to the south. Also the one to find gold first should "telegraph" the news by a discharge of fire arms. Abe Lee and his party took the south gulch and camped in a spot not far from Oro, and at once began their search by panning and after ascertaining the contents of the first pan, Abe Lee shouted, "Boys, this is California", and California it's been ever since.[2]

Although the gulch has proved to be a second California, there is probably no truth to the story, as the distance between the two gulches, California and Colorado, is so great as to make "telegraphing the news by firearms" impossible. Likewise because of the heavy timber, which then covered the region, signal fires could not have been used. News of the rich strike in California Gulch spread rapidly. People began to flock in. Among the early arrivals were Samuel B. Kellogg and H.A. W. Tabor and his wife. Mrs. Tabor was the first woman in camp. She and

....

1 Based on A. Y. Corman, P. G. Goris, and Emmons.

2 This story has been printed by Leadville and Denver newspapers, etc., but its truth is denied by A.Y.Corman and by P. G. Goris.

her husband had started out from Kansas, gone to Denver, Greggory Diggings, then to Arkansas and now to California Gulch. The miners built her a cabin of green pine logs, the roof covered with bark and dirt. She at once began taking boarders, although there was very little to feed them. When the express was established she became post-mistress. The following spring she opened up a store in part of the cabin and while Tabor worked the claim she kept store and boarders. Mrs. Tabor was a fine woman and was loved and respected by the miners. In an interview years later when Tabor was senator, Mrs. Tabor declared, "that in those years of self-sacrifice, hard labor, and economy, she laid the foundation of Mr. Tabor's immense wealth", for had she not stayed with him, and worked by his side he would have become discouraged, returned to his trade and so lost the opportunity which has since enriched him.[1]

Samuel B. Kellogg had already had ten years of placer mining experience in California. He and Tabor reached the present site of Cache Creek and began whip sawing lumber to make sluices for washing the gravel. However a few days later they received news of the discovery of gold in California Gulch. They left Cache Creek, tried prospecting in Iowa Gulch, but with little success, thence to California, where they arrived April 26, and located claims.[2] In May, A. Y. Corman, who afterwards located

....

1 Hill, Colorado Pioneers, P. 218-228. (This account as written by Miss Hill was told her by Mrs. Tabor)

2 Emmons, P. 8-9.

the A.Y. and Minnie and who is still alive, living between Leadville and Malta and hence is probably the earliest prospector still in the locality[1], pitched his tent in the lower part of the gulch. He was on his way to Cherry Creek, but upon striking the mountains learned of the new Eldorado in California Gulch and upon reaching Canon City, joined a party headed for this place. They had to make their own road, and had great difficulty in getting wagons and cattle through, and building a bridge across the Arkansas at Riverside. In spite of difficulties of communication, the news from California Gulch spread with great rapidity and people rushed in from all directions.[2]

By July there were 10,000 people, by August probably 15,000.[3] It is said that $2,000,000 was taken out the first year. This is probably exaggerated, but the record of claims shows tremendous activity. In California Gulch alone 339 claims were located. Fossett writing in 1876 said that many an oyster can of gold nuggetts and gold dust were taken out, and single individuals are said to have carried away fortunes of from $80,000 to $100,000 each. As the result of this summer's labor, Tabor

....

1 Since this was written in the spring of 1916, A. Y. Corman has crossed into the great beyond, perhaps to prepare a place for us as he did at Leadville.

2 A. Y. Corman

3 C. C. Davies, memoirs, P.78, says 60,000, but this is too large.

and Kellogg, working their own claims, made about $75,000 in 60 days. Some claims netted $1000 in a single day. This shows that the California Gulch was the most prosperous and productive camp in the country.[1]

Ovando J. Hollister writing in 1867 declares, California Gulch stands second, if not first, among all the gulches ever worked in Colorado for extent and yield of gold; that the discovery claim produced $60,000 that season; Nos. 5 and 6, above yielded $65,000; No. 1, below, has paid to date $55,000; a large quartz vein runs through Discovery and No. 1 below, from which $216 was sluiced by three men in 1863 in a half day; No. 4, below, prospected from one to ten dollars to the pan on the pay streak, and has produced to date $75,000; No. 5 below has paid $55,000; Nos. 11 and 12 below, paid $26,000; from 13 to 25 the average yield was $10 a day to the hand. Numbers 26 and 27 paid $50,000; nos. 28 to 35 paid $15, and 36 to 41, $25 per day to the man. From 42 to 45 there was no pay, but thence to 56 the average was $18 a day per hand; No. 57 never paid anything, nor did any ground below that, which was but little more than a mile from Discovery; Nos. 14 to 18 paid $20,000 each. Numbers 19 to 20 yielded $80,000 in three months; No. 21 paid $15,000; Nos. 22 to 28, as well as the other claims above Discovery not here specified paid from $3,000 to $5,000 each; from 28 to 36

....

1 A. Y. Corman, P, G. Goris, Emmons, P. 9-10 (Emmons is my authority for statement Tabor & Kellogg took out $75,000, but Miss Hill writes, P. 228, that Mrs. Tabor said that Tabot's claim No. 12 only paid $5,000; the one below it paid $80,000.

the yield gradually fell off; No. 25 paid $15,000; No. 30 paid $6,000; 31 to 35 inclusive did not pay wages; No. 36 paid $3,500; from No. 22 to the head of the gulch occurs a black cement, one to twelve feet thick, too loose to blast to advantage, too hard to be decomposed by water, hydraulics with 100 feet head having no effect upon it.[1]

The usual miner's laws were enforced and the locality had much the same characteristics as the other early mining settlements. There were many saloons, several dance halls and numerous gambling places, at which many a miner played away at night, the rich earnings of the day. Many cabins were built, the principal group extending from the right of what is now Harrison Avenue, eastward to the point of Carbonate Hill, and was known as Oro City, and probably included 200 or 300 cabins, of all sizes, though most of them were small. Besides the gathering at Oro the cabins were scattered from the top of the gulch to where Malta now stands.[2]

The question of food in the gulch was an easy matter; besides the several stores, there were also a great many freighters who brought in supplies and sold them directly from their wagons, and thirdly, game was very plentiful, deer, elk, antelope and mountain sheep covered the hills and it was an easy matter for the miners to stand in their cabin door and shoot a deer or even an elk, while streams, in the words of a '60 man, were "Thick with fish".[3]

....

1 Hollister - Mines of Col. P. 316-317
2, 3 A. Y. Corman, confirmed by Goris.

During this first summer the gulch was worked up as high as Number 20, opposite the Roseman. Number 19 was supposed to be the richest claim. All claims were 100 feet in length, except that a discoverer got two claims; one by discovery and one by preemption, and they were numbered "I" down the gulch, and "I" up.[1]

At the end of this first summer, thousands of miners left the camp and never returned; the great placer days of 1860 were gone forever. Kellogg wandered away into the San Juan region and never returned; Tabor quit mining and went into the store business; the saloons, dance halls, gambling houses, and all the stores but Tabor's gradually left.[2] (Tabor also left between '61 and '68).

For the next three years the mining was carried on by sluices, long tons, Georgia and hand rockers, and pans. Hollister writes in 1867 the claims have now been largely consolidated and mining done by ground sluicing and hydraulics. Thus, W. H. Jones owns and works 1, 2, and 3 below; Leahry & Company, 26 and 27 below, and White Burroughs & Company, 14 to 30 above. The pay streak in these claims yields from $10 to $15 a day per man. Not more than half the gulch is considered worked out. Rich quarts veins traverse it in four or five different places, though these have never received any attention, beyond preempting and sluicing out their dirt crevices, some of which paid extraordinarily. A tunnel called the "Bury Tunnel" at the head of the gulch, discovers a short distance from its mouth, a strong vein of excellent ore. Although a few parties still make enough to support them through the winter by working

in the gulch in the summer, its future prosperity, and this is true of the entire county, must depend on the development of the quartz mines.[1]

Horace Greeley had contributed greatly to the gold rush to Colorado in 1860 by his newspaper writings. It seems that Greeley was returning home from California when he heard of the gold strike in Colorado; he immediately went to the Gregory diggings and investigated personally. The miners gave him a royal welcome, but meanwhile a few of the boys had taken an old shot gun and fired gold dust into a hole for all it was worth. Then Mr. Greeley, accompanied or rather lead, by some of the most plausible and versatile talkers, was escorted over the diggings and was told of all the interesting events in the history of its discovery and was shown specimens of the dirt and of the pure gold that had been washed out. Greeley called for a shovel and pans and rolled up his sleeves and went down into the pit. They gave him all the necessary instructions as to the process of panning, and looked on with palpitating anxiety. Mr. Greeley was an apt scholar and put his dirt through with rare skill. It panned out big. All the bottom of the pan was covered with bright gold particles. They slapped him on the shoulders in regular Western style, and told him to try it again, which he did with the same success. Then gathering up his gold dust he

....

[1] Ovando J. Hollister, The Mines of Colorado, P. 317-318

exclaimed, "Gentlemen, I have worked with my own hands and have seen with my own eyes, and the news of your rich discovery shall go over the world, as far as my paper can waft it.". Upon his return to New York City he devoted an entire page of the Tribune to an ecstatic description of the camp and continued to shout into the ears of the crowded East the words, "Young man, go West".[1]

Count Murat, a Colorado barber, feeling he would be distinguished by a notice from the great journalist, and also wishing to impress him with the liberal product of the gold fields, charged Mr. Greeley two dollars for a single shave. This also, perhaps, helped Mr. Greeley reach his decision regarding the desirability of going West.[2]

Up to 1860 Auraria was the leading town in Colorado, although the Pike's Peak Express Company had changed their headquarters to Denver, having received 1,460 town lots for so doing. In the spring of 1860 Auraria, Denver, and Highland consolidated under the name of Denver.[3]

Congress organized the Territory of Colorado, February 26, 1861. The first Governor was Wm. Gilpin, followed the following year by John Evans, H. P. Bennett was the first delegate to Congress.[4] The first territorial legislature met at Twin Lakes in the summer of 1864 and it adjourned to Golden.[5] In the summer

....

1 and 2
Hill, Pages 30 and 31
3 Fossett, P. 40
4 History of Arkansas Valley - (Baskins & Co.) P. 207
5 C. H. S. Whipple - Con Cunningham

of 1861, Lake County was organized by proclamation of Governor Gilpin. It included all of the present counties of Lake, Pitkin, Mesa, Delta, Gunnison, Chaffee, Montrose, Ouray, San Miguel, most of Dolores, part of Montezuma, San Juan, Hinsdale, Mineral, and Saguache. It held these boundaries until 1874, when three new counties were erected in the southwestern part of the territory at the expense of Conejos and Lake. In 1877 Gunnison was cut from the western half of Lake, and again two years later, 1879, during the excitement over the Carbonates and the rush to Leadsville, the legislature divided the county in two, giving the north half the name of Carbonate, and the southern half Chaffee, but before the end of the session, the name Carbonate was discarded for the old name of Lake, and the county has held these boundaries ever since.[1]

In the fall of 1861 an election was held and Captain Breece, Alexander McPherson and Wm. Snyder were chosen county commissioners, and Eli Blair sheriff, with Col. Austin probate judge.[2]

During the fall of 1861 a good many southerners left California Gulch to join the Confederate Army. A few northern miners joined the first Colorado regiment, but enough remained to make the Gulch intensely loyal to the Union. There was considerable gossip that if the southerners could get Colorado to

....

1 F.L.Paxson - The County Boundaries of Colorado. In Univ. of Col. Studies, Vol. III, Pages 199-215.

2 History of Arkansas Valley - (Baskins & Co.),Chicago, 1881, Page 207

join the Confederacy they would seize Denver, etc. These stories exsited the Unionists to such an extent that when the news came that a neighboring gulch was flying the Confederate flags, they organized 2,000 armed men and prepared to march to rescue Denver and the state. Later, however, they learned that Denver and the state were safe; then a warning was sent to the neighboring gulch, and the matter was closed without blood-shed.[1]

During the summer of this year a ditch called the Eldorado was built from Evans Gulch to aid in carrying on the sluice mining, but owing to the great cost of supplies which had to be "freighted in" only the richest gravel could be worked, and little attention was paid to vein deposites. Few suspected the real wealth of the region, although the miners were much annoyed in their work by iron-stained fragments of heavy rock which they had to throw out of the sluices by hand. This ditch changed hands several times, but was finally secured by John Lahey and Tom Starr, the latter, who came in 1862 located claim 255, or Starr's Placer, which is probably the best known placer claim. He worked this claim for twenty years and it netted $7,000 per year.[2]

Starr built in the early 60's the house in the gulch now occupied by Mrs. Starr and Mr. Cunningham. This house, one of the oldest in the county, is located on very valuable ground,

....

1 History of Arkansas Valley - P. 214

2 By Con Cunningham, confirmed by Mrs, Starr and A.Y.Corman.

Starr at one time refusing $75,000 for it. Starr was one of the best known, and best liked men in the camp. It is related that during one severe winter in early days, he carried a sack of flour, for which he paid $75, over Mosquito range on snow shoes, and when he reached home, finding his fellow miners without bread, cheerfully divided his flour with them and refused to take any pay. Starr enlarged and improved the Eldorado ditch, and it has ever since been known as Starr's ditch, and the water privilege is still controlled by his estate.[1]

Abe Lee was elected recorder for the camp and used his fees to erect the first house in Leadville. Prices were high during this period; lumber was in great demand, and sold at twenty-five cents per foot; flour was one dollar a pound, and sugar still higher.[2]

The only man killed by the miners during the early days, although there were occasional shooting scraps, was one named Kennedy. The mining laws prohibited the taking up of claims by proxy, but Kennedy determined to take one for his son-in-law back in the states, and hold it with a shot gun. Two other men recorded the claim and decided to take it. Kennedy threatened to shot them, but one of them fired first. He was tried by the miners, but acquitted.[3]

....

1 By Con Cunningham, confirmed by Mrs. Starr and A.Y.Corman
2 History of Arkansas Valley, P. 213.
3 History of Arkansas Valley, P. 213.

In 1861, also occured the Espinosa affair. A great number of men had been found mysteriously murdered on the public roads, etc. This created great excitement. Confederate guerrillas were at first suspected. A company was formed which later discovered two Mexicans; they opened fire; one was killed, the other escaped, but was killed later. From papers found in their camp it was learned that they were two cousins named Espinosa, and that they had declared war upon the United States and had already killed forty men.[1]

There are a great many interesting stories told of this early period in California Gulch. Alice Polk Hill, in her book on the Colorado Pioneers, tells several as follows: One of them is about a miner named Pat Smith who struck it rich and hence had honors thrust upon him. He was nominated for Justice of the Peace, although he had never read a line of law in his life. Jim Brown, a lawyer well up in his profession, declared he didn't want to practice before such an ignoramus as Smith, and fought him with might and main during the canvass. However, Smith was elected and lost no opportunity to get even with Brown. On one occasion a man was seen going on one of the lonely highways at a rapid gait on a horse that belonged to someone else. The owner brought suit to recover his property. Brown was engaged by the defense and brought up points of law to convince the Justice that the man being in possession of the

....

[1] History of Arkansas Valley, P. 214.

horse was not proof positive that he had stolen it. Smith instantly overruled all these points, and finally Brown read from Blackstone a case precisely similar to the one before the court. "What do I care for Blackstone or any other lawyer", cried Smith, "I know the man stole the horse and I have decided, that's enough. I am Judge here, sir". "Your honor" replied Brown, "I know you have decided the case. I read the point merely to show you - old fool -". "What's that?" interrupted the court, springing to his feet in a frenzied rage. "Blackstone was", calmly concluded the laywer resuming his seat.[1]

Another story is told of a politician who struck the gulch and desired to address the miners. A dry-goods box was placed in front of "Aunt Betsy's", a hotel at the mouth of the gulch, and a large crowd gathered. In the midst of a grand oratorical flight, a disturbance commenced in the edge of the crowd and gradually spread, as the disturbing cause, which was a small donkey, pushed its way in. The speaker bravely endeavored to maintain himself against the uproar, but in vain. The animal, which belonged to the landlady, was accustomed to be fed at the hotel steps, at this hour, and wasmaking his way in to receive his rations as usual. The crowd parted before him. He marched directly up to the platform, fixed his melancholy eye on the speaker and gave vent to a discordant "hee haw, hee haw" that arose the echoes from the surrounding hills. The politician bowing to his audience said, "One at a time, gentlemen". The

....

[1] Hill, - Pages 210-211.

crowd laughed in uproarious laughter and this is probably the only time that a political meeting was ever broken up by a bona fide four-legged jack-ass.[1]

A third story is that of a young gospel dispenser who made his way into camp and announced his intention about preaching, but was advised to leave by some of the worst characters in camp; but one of the most reckless of adventurers, "Devil Dick", declared himself the minister's champion. On the day and hour set for the sermon, he appeared and delivered himself with the following:

"Friends and gentlemen, listen to me. I was the first American to cross the Great Desert, the first to visit the sacred spot where the Sainted Montezuma, the Indian Savior, mounted upon the back of the glorious white eagle, to take his flight heavenward, and I hope to be here when he returns to take his people home.

"I was here when the pilgrims came hunting gold in this glorious land. I was here when the first American woman arrived, 'God Bless her'. I was here when the bad men first opened their dens of iniquity; when that poor boy's soul took its flight across the range for refusing to play poker with Bill Sykes, for he said he promised his good old mother never to gamble. This was my first sin, but I had to do it. I sent Bill to 'Kingdom Come' by limited express. Bucksin Joe soon followed Bill. I had to do it. Seven-up Pete went next; I had to do that too'. Now, I becamed a marked man. Some called me bad, but I was

....

1 Hill, P. 211-212.

always on the side of the weak and helpless. Since then I have had some pretty lively times; have been a prospector, miner, Government Scout, cow-boy, stage driver, and trapper, and between times amused myself gunning for Indians and Greasers on my own account. Yes, I have been handled pretty roughly. I have been 'chased' by grizzlies, scalped by Indians, burned at the stake nearly, shot and knifed dozens of times, blown up once or twice, and on one occasion fell into a quarts mill and ran clean through before I could be stopped.. On another occasion I was dropped in a sluice box and panned out as pure as virgin gold. Now friends, you have said that this beloved minister shall not preach in this camp to a lost and dying world. You have said this, and you come to enforce your threat, you carry your guns, knives, and sabers, and come equipped with all this arsenal; for what? Simply to bluff this defenseless unarmed minister of the gospel who means you only good. But there is no bluff in this game. I hold four aces and the five spot and the first man that moves, I'll raise him. Boys, I mean business. You know me of old; you'll hear the Gospel; you'll hear it now!" Then laying down his navy six-shooter on the pine table, used for a pulpit, he turned to the minister, saying in his most persuasive way, "Parson sail in. Give'em H--l. I'll back you".[1]

After 1861, the population in the gulch dwindled away rapidly. By 1866, there were only 152 people in the whole country, and the county then included everything from the summit of Mosquito range to the southern part of the state. Production also fell off rapidly. After 1866 it was very light; the

....

[1] Hill - P. 212-215.

placers in 1869 produced only $60,000, and by 1876 but $20,000, and for ten years there was not a lawsuit in the whole county. The camp was pretty dead by the middle of the 60's.[1]

In 1867 Hollister writes "California Gulch is now almost deserted. The relics of former life and business - old boots and clothes, cooking utensils, rude house furniture, tin cans, gold pans, wornout shovels and picks, and the remains of towns, half buried sluices and rifle boxes, dirted-roofed cabins tumbling down, and the county turned inside out and disguised with the rubbish of every description, are most disagreeably abundant and suggestive."[2] Ned E. Farrell, writing about the same time, said"the rich placers have been exhausted and business is prostrate".[3]

And it was during this period that a Denver merchant remarked, "Tabor is an honest man, and will pay his bills when he can, but what business can he do there. There isn't enough business in Lake County to keep a cat alive, and in order to protect myself, I have limited his account to $50.[4]

Such was the condition of affairs when the Printer Boy, the first gold vein, or lode, was disdovered in June 1868 by Charles J. Mullen and Cooper Smith, who were prospecting for J. Marshall Paul of Philadelphia. (Paul afterwards figured prominently in territorial politics). In August the Boston and Philadelphia

....

1 Gov. A. Y. Corman & P.G.Goris
2 Hollister - Mines of Col., P. 318
3 Ned E. Farrell, Colorado, P. 39
4 History Arkansas Valley, P. 216

Gold and Silver Mining Company of Colorado was organized, and a stampmill erected at Oro to treat the ore from this vein.[1] Major De Mary and others sunk a shaft on the Printer Boy Claims, and took out in the neighborhood of $60,000. The ore was neither smelted nor assayed, but ran through the slices and treated by the old-fashioned Arastra method. This satisfied the Printer Boy people that the claim was valuable, and another shaft was sunk. The two shafts were known as the upper and lower Printer Boy shafts. It was in the spring of 1867 that Charles L. Hill took charge and in fourteen months, with but thirty men working, he took out $116,000 in gold. The vein was 20 inches wide. It was decomposed porphyry and iron, of a clayed consistency, the walls being of pyritifuous or grey porphyry. The mine was in many respects quite remarkable, and some wonderful pockets of rich mineral were opened up. One evening three of the men came down to Mr. Hill's cabin with three ordinary sacks of ore calculated to hold fifty pounds each. Before washing the dirt, Mr. Hill picked out 110 ounces of coarse gold, one nugget weighing six ounces. The washing yielded 50 ounces more, making 160 ounces from 150 pounds, the whole being valued at $3,200.[2] The Printer Boy was the bonanza section of the whole country, but it did not create intense excitement. The Five-Twenty was opened up and paying. The Lincoln was on the shipping list, and the

....

1 Emmons, P. 10

2 It is claimed the mine produced in all between $600,000 to $800,000, but perhaps this is rather high.

Lower Printer Boy was considered next to the Printer Boy in point of value. It was owned by Captain Breece and Joseph and Thomas Wells. One lot of amalgam taken to Denver weighed 60 pounds. Ben. Bernard & Company were working the Pilot. They took out a single pan that yielded 30 ounces of the precious metal, and Mr. Bernard reaped a rich harvest from this property.[1] These workings were carried on more or less continuously until 1877, and at times imparted a fitful prosperity, but never the stampede of 1860. People knew by this time that all who came west would not become millionaires.[2]

Meanwhile the site of Oro had been changed several times. At first scattered along the Gulch, then concentrated at the mouth, very near present Leadville, then moved up by the stamp-mill. This later place was called New Oro. Tabor moved his store up here and was also postmaster. A school was organized as District No. 1, and a building erected near the Moyer Shaft in 1872. At this time Old Joe Pierce was running a hotel at New Oro. The first Odd Fellow's Hall was built the same year as the school. It was a log building, 45 feet by 20 feet. The lower portion was used as a house, and the upper part as a hall and an assembly room. The business section was down about 300 feet from the hall. There were two saloons, run by McDermott

....

1 Statement by Charles L. Hill in Leadville Gold Belt (Compiled by C.H.Morse) P. 23-24.

2 A. Y. Corman, confirmed by P.G.Goris & Con Cunningham.

and Gilmore respectively, both started in 1872. Mr. McDermott had been in the gulch at an earlier date, had gone to New Mexico and lost his arm and upon his return to New Oro, the boys "chipped in" and set him up in the saloon business.[1]

Things were pretty quiet through this period, and by 1875 there were only two or three hundred people in the entire gulch. Placer mining had almost died out and the camp, like the placer mining, would soon have come to an end but for the discovery of the Carbonates.[2]

....

1 and 2
P. G. Goris - confirmed by Con Cunningham and A.Y.Corman.

CHAPTER II

THE DISCOVERY OF THE CARBONATES

All through the "Placer Period" the placer miner had been bothered by iron stained rocks that he was forced to throw out by hand and by heavy sand that he cursed because it blocked up his sluice boxes. Few of them had any idea what these rocks and "heavy sand" really were, while apparently none appreciated their great potential value.

There is a report that in August 1861, C. M. Rouse and C.H. Cameron of Madison, Wisconsin, "struck" carbonates of which a small quantity was shipped to George T. Clark of Denver, and that samples which he sent to Chicago yielded by assay 164 ounces of silver to the ton. The Washoi Mining Company was founded on these discoveries, but no work done, and even the location of its claims is forgotten.[1]

There are a number of interesting stories told of the miners during the "60's", that show their complete ignorance of the great value of the quantities of carbonates so close at hand. One of the best told by A.Y.Corman, who later located the A.Y. and Minnie, is as follows:

In 1866 a prospector struck the camp and worked hard at digging a hole in the gulch across from Corman's cabin and about where the Dome mine is located today. Corman, who had worked on this place himself, did not want to discourage him, but told him the "stuff" was no good. However, the prospector kept at it, and suddenly one day disappeared. Corman, with

....

[1]Emmons, P. 10.

whom he had been boarding, was greatly worried and looked all over the camp for him, but not a sign of him was to be found. But late in the Fall the prospector drove up to Corman's door with a great load of apples. He asked Corman if he wanted some; Corman bought what he could use, then asked the prospector why he had disappeared. The fellow told him that he had struck some fine looking stuff in his "mine" and had taken samples to Denver to be assayed. (There was no assayer in camp at that time).

"Well, what was in the stuff?"

"It wasn't worth a d---" , replied the prospector. "Ran 70% lead and 11 ounces of silver. Come over and I will show you the place. You can have it; I don't want it".

"Neither do I", said Corman,"I worked there before you did".[1]

A second story is that of the early timer that used this black sand, not realizing that it was rich in silver,to bank up the sides of his cabin. Another miner used some of this sand to make mortar for a fire place, and the sand ran so heavy in lead that when the fire place was completed, and the fire built, the lead melted out between the bricks and ran down the sides.[2]

The first carbonate was recognized by Mike Norris on Mike Lode in 1868. Some few years later, 1871, the Homestake Silver Mine in the Sawatch Range, opposite the head waters of the

....

[1] A.Y.Corman

[2] P.G.Goris, and Con Cunningham.

Arkansas, was discovered by McFadden, Crawford Bros., and Carney. They gave it this name because they hoped to make enough so they could quit and go home. It proved rich beyond the most sanguine expectations. The discovers sold it to Colonel Archer, millionaire owner of the Denver water works and gas system, but whose fortune was laid by the out-put of the Old Homestake. The discovery of this mine caused a stampede to Homestake Gulch. No one was left in Oro. Later in 1876 a smelter was erected at Malta to treat the ore from this mine.[1]

The real credit of realizing the value of the carbonates deposits belongs principally to A.B.Wood and W.H.Stevens. Wood came to California Gulch in April 1874 to work Tom Starr's placer claim, and together with Stevens started early that summer the construction of a twelve mile ditch afterwards known as Lieter's Ditch, to bring more water into California Gulch. Their plan was to bring in enough water to permit hydraulic mining and the cheap handling of unworked gravel banks. The work took several years and was done by what was called the Oro Ditch and Fluming Company.[2]

Soon after the ditch was started Stevens brought in sixteen Chinamen to work upon it. Now the miners living at Oro in the Gulch resented the importation of foreign labor and a party led by P.G.Goris, one of the young leaders and also considered the best boxer in the camp, proceeded up to the "Ditch" and tried to induse the Chinamen to leave. Only a few of the party carried fire arms, but it was easy to persuade the Chinamen to pack up

....
1 P.G.Goris, Con Cunningham, and Emmons, P. 11
2 Con Cunningham, and Emmons, P. 11.

their bundles and leave; however, it was more difficult to locate all the victims as some took to the woods. They were shut up in a cabin and arrangements made to take them to Fairplay, but the Chinese fearing a lack of fair play left before the team provided by the miners was ready. Wm. Musgrove had been in charge of the Chinese; he tried to resist the miners, and later had warrants sworn out for them. McKay, local constable, made the arrest, and he took Goris and eleven other men to Granite for trial. On the way down the twelve prisoners secretly robbed him of his pistols and weapons. Preliminary trial was held before Justice of Peace Charles Mater. (Mater later came to Leadville and opened the first store on Chestnut Street). Old Judge Huton was the lawyer for the defense. A.S.Weston was prosecuting attorney. Mater bound over the twelve prisoners to the District Course, and put them under $100 bonds each, but the miners refused to pay up and said they all wanted to go to jail.[1]

John Welldon was sheriff and had absolutely no place to keep so many prisoners. He tried to get them to go each others bond, but they refused; thereupon he turned them loose. However, all showed up at the District Court without trouble; they even paid their own fare and saved the county every expense. The case was known as State Vs. P.G. Goris, et. el. The trial was held at Granite, August 1874, in the Masonic Hall over Kraft's old store. There was great difficulty in securing a jury. Old

....

1 Practically as recited by Goris to me. Later substantiated by Cunningham. Cunningham was in the camp at the time, but did not participate in the affair.

Judge Miller represented the miners this time. The trial lasted several days; the jury was out about five hours, and returned with the verdict of acquittal; only one wanted to convict. Judge Wells in discharging the twelve defendents became sarcastic and told them to go back to California Gulch and drive out all the Chinese or anybody else they didn't like or want. Other men connected with Goris in this case were J.M.Calvert, N.A.Rich, Wm. McDermith, Dick Street, etc. Later during the "Rush Days" a Chinamen named R. Kan came to Leadville from Alma to start a laundry, but the boys threw rocks at him and he soon left. These are the only two occasions when Chinese ever came into the great carbonate camp.[1]

To return to Wood and Stevens, we find that Wood was greatly impressed by the heavy rock and gravel that stuck in the sluices. He assayed some, but his specimens were not rich,yielding only 27% lead and 15 ounces of silver to the ton. However, he put prospectors to work to locate the croppings of the ore deposit and in June 1874 carbonate in place was located on Dome Hill; Bradshaw had also sunk a shaft and struck ore on the Ora La Plata Claim about the same time. In the spring of 1875 Wood, Stevens, and Professor H. Bergher located the Lime, Rock and Dome Claims, and then during the summer they located over on Iron Hill for Detroit parties the Iron, which now constitutes the

....

1 Practically as recited by Goris to me. Later substantiated by Cunningham. Cunningham was in the camp at the time but did not participate in the affair.

valuable property of the Iron Silver Mining Company. Wood made most of his money out of this mine.[1] Sometime later Stevens went to Detroit and brought out a gang of men to work these claims. They were known as the Detroiters, but very soon got tired of the camp and work. They demanded money in order to pay their way back to Detroit, and when it was not immediately forthcoming, theythreatened to hang Stevens. Finally they arranged that he be held a prisoner in Tabor's store while a messenger named Al Lee was sent to Fairplay to secure money from Hathaway's bankto enable Wood to pay their way back to Detroit. When the money arrived, most of them left camp for good.[2]

In 1875"Best Friend" was located by Joseph Doyle and Long and Derry located the mine of that name the following year. Also in 1876, A.R. Meyers, a graduate of European Mining Schools, sent 200 or 300 tons of ore principally from the Rock Mine, by wagon to Colorado Springs, and hence by rail to St. Louis. It cost $25 per ton to get it to Colorado Springs and the ore only averaged seven ounces of silver to the ton, but it ran 60% lead, and owing to the high price of lead (seven cents a pound) netted a profit. This proved that the Leadville Mines could profitably be worked.[3]

Prospecting continued; the Adelaide was located this year by Walls and Powers, and proved to be a good producer. The Camp

....

1 Emmons, P. 11-12.

2 Con Cunningham, Mrs.Starr.- A heavy snow storm in May seems to have been the cause of the Detroiters' dissatisfaction.

3 Con Cunningham and Emmons, P. 12.

Bird, another early discovery, was opened up by the Gallagher Bros. Up to 1876 all the claims located were situated on Iron and Rock Hills in California Gulch. In 1877 mineral was discovered on Carbonate Hill and a number of claims located, while the following year the New Discovery was located on Fryer Hill by George Fryer.[1]

This was followed, May 1, 1878, by the most important discovery of all; namely, the Little Pittsburgh. It seems that one day two Pittsburgh shoe makers, named Hook and Risch, who knew absolutely nothing of mining, struck California Gulch and asked Tabor if he would grub stake them. Tabor had a habit of granting most everything; hence, provided the men with a liberal supply of provisions and a jug of whiskey. And it was this jug of whiskey that made Tabor, for we find that his new prospectors set out across the ridges, but as it was a warm day and their remembrance of the jog of whiskey was strong, they got no further than Fryer Hill, when they decided to seek a comfortable spot and to enjoy the liquid; and under the influence of this, they concluded that that particular spot was as convenient a place as any other for sinking a shaft. They struck ore at about 25 or 30 feet. Although it is the only point on the entire hill where ore is as near to the surface. The mine was named the "Little Pittsburgh" and proved to be a wonder. Nearly $5,000,000 was produced in two years.[2] It made a millionaire out of Tabor,

....

[1]P.G.Goris, Con Cunningham, and History of Arkansas Valley, P.218

[2]This story has been quoted in many places and with many minor variations, but usually the same regarding essential facts.

although we find that his fortune was greatly increased in a very singular way.

His commission house in Denver of whom he bought his supplies, upon learning of the great strikes being made in this region asked him to purchase some mining property for them. Tabor bought, in response to this request, a claim from Chicken Bill (property now known as the Chrysolite) for $2,500, not knowing that Chicken Bill had, instead of striking ore, simply salted it with samples from the Little Pittsburgh. Upon receiving his money Chicken Bill immediately went to Denver to spend it, and while in Denver told his friends the whole affair. The story immediately leaked out and reached the commission house before they had received the property from Tabor. The result was that Tabor had to keep it. He now formed an association under title of Tabor, Borden and Company. They bought up adjoining claims and developed the place. They took out about $1,500,000 and then sold to the Chrysolite Company for another $1,500,000.[1]

The history of this transaction has been made the subject of an entertaining bit of poetry by F.E.Vaughn of Leadville, and was printed first in the Leadville Herald Democrat and later in the Souvenir of the Elk's Convention held in Leadville June 1907. The poem is as follows:

....

[1] This is substantially the story as told by Emmons, P. 15, but he gives the amount as $40,000. Local tradition varies greatly as to the amount paid, but $2,500 is a very likely figure.

Of course you have read of the wicked ways
Of Leadville town in the early days,
Of the "killers" and "grafters" who lived here when
The place was peopled by gambling men,
When it cost a fortune to eat and sleep
When life and morals both were cheap,
And one owned all one could get and keep.

Men who had sifted the golden sand
From the mountain peaks of many lands,
Capitalist, criminal, tenderfoot, tramp,
All drifted into the silver camp.
By luck, design, or by God's will,
There lived in a shack on Fryer Hill
A prospector known as Chicken Bill.

This was way back in seventy-nine
When every claim was a paying mine,
When money and suckers both were thick
And prospectors sold without a stroke of pick,
Then the boys and the camp were thoroughbred
One got drunk and painted the other red
And maybe wound up half filled with lead.

This Chicken Bill was a queer old cuss
Who worked away without making a fuss,
Sinking a hole into Fryer Hill
With pick, and shovel, and iron will.
But he had a mild and simple look
And a face you could read like an open book
With a hand shake that couldn't be mistook.

Bill's shaft was down some seventy feet
In a wash formation hard to beat
With one man twisting an old "armstrong"
His work was hard and his hours were long.
When Hook, Rische, and Tabor found
The Pittsburgh Bonanza lying around
With dollars almost on top of the ground.

Old Chicken Bill went down to look
At the prospect opened by Rische and Hook
Chloride ore of the finest kind,
And every seam was "shamrock""lined.
He looked it over and opened his eyes
At sight of the dazzling silver prise
But he said nothing -- for Bill was wise.

That night as he lay in his lonely bed
On the old hill side in the dirt thatched shed
A brilliant thought flashed through his brain
Which he sifted over and over again
For Bill had learned in by-gone days
Sundry and various crooked ways,
And he said, "Everything is right that pays".

Three shifts were working on the jump
Piling the ore on the Pittsburg dump,
Thousands of dollars were lying there
And millions more below to spare.
Bill took a few sacks of Pittsburg ore
Just what he needed -- not a bit more,
It was never missed from the bountiful store.

Things were "doin" 'round his shaft that night
In the pallid glare of the old moon's light,
And when he had finished he softly laughed,
There was lots of ore in old Bill's shaft,
Ore on the dump and lying around,
Ore like the Little Pittsburgh found,
Ore on the top and underground.

Next day when Tabor came on the hill
He went to see old Chicken Bill
He found him sitting on the dump
With a microscope and a d---- rich lump.
Now Tabor didn't know it all
But it was a big bluff he wouldn't call,
So he bought out Chicken Bill -- that's all.

Nine hundred dollars, so they say
Was the price that Tabor had to pay
(I may be wrong, or I may be right)
For a quit claim deed to the Chrysolite.
Out of the country went Chicken Bill
Leaving Tabor with mighty good will
And the "wash" hole up on Fryer Hill.

Some stories have sequels, so they say
And when Tabor went up the following day
He wasn't feeling so very fine
For he found he had purchased a salted mine.
Salted as I have said before
From the Pittsburg dump with Tabor ore
'Twas enough to make a man feel sore.

But Tabor had money, and Tabor had sand
With a world of faith at his command,
He put that shaft down ten feet more
And this time Tabor got the ore.
Three million was what he made
After the trick the smooth man played
That was because he always "stayed".

Now just a few words about Tabor's ways
From those who knew him in by gone days.
His heart and bank account were big
He stood by his friends and didn't renige,
He was the man who won renown
By making a city of Denver town
Before the parasites threw him down.

Times have changed -- hair turned gray,
And many old timers have passed away
The bad man has gone to his final rest
From the silver camp of the golden west
Exit Tabor and Chicken Bill
But over there is Fryer Hill
Quietly producing millions still."

The discovery of the Little Pittsburgh now brings our history of Leadville up to the marvelous happenings of the Rush Days, but before leaving this period there are several things I wish to mention.

One is the extremely small population throughout this entire period. At no one time from the early sixties until the late spring of 1876 was there probably more than 300 people in the entire region. Tabor ran the only store. His main store was situated in California Gulch, above Starr's claim, with a branch at Malta. Bifield started a store at one time in this period but it did not last long. There were but two saloons. Dance halls were scarce, since the "Old Timers" tell us that A.Y.Corman was the only fiddler in the camp, and that he could play but three tunes, of which the "Irish Wash Woman" was the most popular. P.G.Goris was considered the best dancer in the district. Also there was very little crime and practically no excitement.[1]

....

[1] Con Cunningham, confirmed by Mrs. Starr.

About the only affair that is important enough to mention was the shooting of DeMore by Pat Murphy, early in 1874. All the boys would go down to McDermotts' saloon on Saturday evening. All had money and they usually played poker, and as there were not enough tables, they sat on a blanket on the floor. It happened that Pat Murphy pulled out a big bag of money in order to buy chips. DeMore noticed the large amount of money carried by Murphy, proceeded to fill him up, then took him home and put him to bed. After he supposed Murphy asleep he proceed to rob him, but Murphy, only in a stupor, realized where his money had gone to. Next day DeMore went to Granite to have a tooth pulled, but this was only a bluff, and while there engaged in a poker game, showed $20 bills pretty freely. This confirmed Murphy's suspicions, who sometime later accused him in McDermott's saloon of stealing his money. DeMore denied this, but Murphy put a pistol to his head and fired. His preliminary trial was held before Justice of the Peace James Tisdell. Weston was the prosecuting attorney. Murphy was bound over to the District Course, and in the mean time placed in a cabin in the gulch with a guard to watch him. Mike Norris got the guard full and some of the fellows took the sash out of the window and persuaded Murphy to leave. They took him up to the Printer Boy where they had snow shoes hidden, and from here he and a guide crossed the range on snow shoes to Fairplay and he has never been heard of since.[1]

....

[1] P.G.Goris, Con Cunningham, confirmed by James R.McNaece,with the exception that McNaece says Murphy returned to the region during the Rush Days and was engaged in the mining of the Carbonates.

Holdups also were almost unknown until the Rush Days. However, in 1875 and 1876 there was a great deal of disturbance caused by cattle thieves, who committed a great number of outrages, murders, etc. It became necessary for the people to organize in order to rid themselves of the thieves, and a number of people were killed on both sides, including the county judge who was shot while sitting on the bench presiding at a trial connected with the cattle thieves. After this affair things were pretty quiet again until after the discovery of the Little Pittsburgh.[1]

The camp was really a desolate place. It was near the end of this period that Fred Conant of Colorado Springs Gazette visited Stevens, and after viewing the entire region told Stevens he wouldn't take it as a gift. Stevens replied that within a few years it would be the most wonderful mining camp in the world.[2]

But even as late as December 1877 we find that there was little real knowledge of the value of the carbonates as shown by the following letter written by Tabor, December 20, 1877, to L.A.Kent of Denver: "Your letter has just been received and in reply I beg leave to state that owing to some excitement regarding carbonates the placer mines have been neglected, but as near as I can estimate the product in round numbers will be $100,000.[3]

....

[1]Hall, History of Colorado, Vol.II, P.427, and Con Cunningham.
[2]History Arkansas Valley, P. 218
[3]James M. Knight (former newspaper owner) in Elk's Convention, Pamphlet, June 1907.

CHAPTER III

THE RUSH DAYS

With the discovery of the "Little Pittsburgh", May 1, 1878, the real rush began and never before in world's history, with the possible exception of the gold rush to California in 1849, was there such a rush. People streamed into the new carbonate camp by the thousands. The reports of the "Little Pittsburgh" created tremendous excitement, and resulted in a regular stampede to the land of promise.

"The seekers after fortunes came in veritable armies. In every city of the state there were those whose means had been ground well-nigh to nothingness in the contracting, pinching times succeeding the great panic of 1873. These, with rekindled hopes and reanimated energies, hastened to grasp the opportunities afforded by the new city in the mountains. Those, who in their old places, had come to the end of their purposing and planning only to find nothing, started out to commence again in the new land of promise. Those who had searched in vain throughout all the older gold and silver bearing territories, shouldered their picks to make one more trial among the carbonate hills. The hopeful came to improve the great opportunity. The despairing followed to try one more chance. The calculating and prudent came to build up solidly. The desperate and reckless rushed in to gather rapidly. It was a strangely mixed crowd that climb-

ed over the mountain ranges to the carbonate settlement in the Arkansas Valley. The skilled prospector, the novice in knowledge of lodes, the hardened miner, the soft-skinned clerk, the spectacled scientist, the noisy mule driver, the broken-down merchant, the briefless lawyer, the patientless doctor, the baffled speculator, the sold-out real estate owner, the eager gambler, the calculating dealer, the crafty faro man, the designing boarding-housekeeper, the enterprising dance hall man, the pretentious expert, the rough laborer and the delicate gentlemen, all mingled together in the tumultous, rushing crowd, And the devoted clergyman, the earnest teacher, and the ambitious journalist followed hard after."[1]

Such was the crowd that poured into the new discovery, first from every mining camp and city in the state, then from every state in the Union, and lastly from every country in the world, but the orient, for in this jamming mass the lesson taught by Goris et el in 1874 was not forgotten by the yellow-skinned laborer.[2] The seekers of wealth came in by thousands; many stayed only a few days, but there were always more to take their places.[3]

In 1877 there had not been more than 200 or 300 in the entire camp, but within a short period it rose to be the second largest city in the state with a population of 15,000; the rush started in the summer of '78, and grew mightier throughout '79

....

[1] From the Leadville Chronicle of Jan. 1, 1881

[2 and 3] James M. Knight, confirmed by others.

and the spring of '80. Probably from the discovery of the "Little Pittsburgh" to the fall of 1880 not less than 200,000 people poured into the world's greatest mining camp. It is estimated that in the winter of 1879 and the spring of 1880 not fewer than 35,000 people lived in Leadville and the adjoining hills. As many as twenty stage coaches arrived in a day and the average was fourteen. Every one came loaded to the limit and then some. The passengers cared little how they arrived, as long as they got to the carbonate camp.[1]

In June of 1877 Charles Mater had moved from Granite and erected a store building on what is now Chestnut. Before he actually commenced business, Tabor moved his store from Oro to the corner of Chestnut and Harrison. Other buildings followed rapidly. By the fall of 1878 Chestnut Street was the thriving center of saloons, dance halls, faro dens, and hotels. The avenue, called after Harrison of the reduction works, was laid out that fall. Later it was paved with slag from the smelter, and since the smelting of that day was very crude, the slag contained a great amount of silver and furnished the basis for the story that Harrison Avenue is paved with silver. Soon buildings began to be put up on Harrison Avenue. The first one was erected by the Chronicle about two blocks above Chestnut, and was a frame building about twenty by thirty feet. Other buildings followed rapidly. The year 1879 was remarkable for its rapid building. People erected with frenzy. In the morning

....

[1]History Arkansas Valley, P. 237. James Knight's Elks Convention Pamphlet. Other authorities claim even more; for example, Davis, P. 111, says 60,000 at one time. This is certainly too high.

a lot would be vacant; by night fall a complete structure would be raised on the same, with the owner ready to hold his possession with a shot gun. Whole blocks grew up in less than a week.[1]

Early in the history of Leadville, and before it had been dignified with a name, the St. Louis Smelting and Refining Company amended an application for a pending placer claim, higher up the gulch, surveying a narrow strip along the water line to a point sufficiently wide and level to accommodate a good-sized city. This was platted, and the meager little subdivisions sold to the pioneers at excessive figures, as the town began to expand. This obvious perversion of the intent of the federal mining laws secured by means of untruthful declarations regarding "mineral in place" was nevertheless subsequently sustained by the Supreme Court, and it enabled the owners of the patent to hold up lot buyers from the very inception of the town.[2]

The plateau upon which the city sprang up rises ten or twelve thousand feet above the sea. To the East rises Carbonate and Iron Hills, and Ball Mountains to a height of 14,000 feet. These were "the main treasure chest of the Leadville District."[3]

Cal Davis, the founder of the Leadville Chronicle and formerly the greatest newspaper man in the west writes: "The soil upon which it (Leadville) is built is almost as barren as the lava beds of Arizona. Stunted pines, with an occasional scrub

....

1James Knight, Con Cunningham, Judge Cavender, and others.
2Davis, P. 110-111.
3Davis, P. 111.

oak, alone varied the unattractive landscape. Untold wealth lay buried below the surface; above it naught was found to sustain life."[1]

It is true that the wonderful mining prospect was the thing that brought this mass of men to Leadville, but mining was a long way from being the major activity in 1879. Building, buying, selling or jumping claims, and gambling all engaged more attention than actual mining itself.[2]

By April 1879 the boom had fairly begun, but more continued to crowd in and notwithstanding the increased accommodations it was almost impossible to secure shelter. Men paid a dollar a piece for the privilege of sleeping on a billiard table, others bought up the chair privilege in a saloon. T.R.Agnew, at one time candidate for mayor in New York City, early in 1879 brought in a riff-raff collection of lumber and erected a biz bain as lodging house in the second block of west Chestnut. Here there were three tiers of bunks with calico curtains in front. Every night each bunk was worth one dollar to the eccentric Agnew, who insisted that only mayors of great cities and govenors could sleep in the lower berths.[3]

Tabor had built a great building in 1878 below the O.K. saloon on Chestnut known as the Wigwam. This had been erected as a place for political meetings. The most notable one ever held there was the debate between James B. Belford and T. M.

....

1 Davis, P. 111
2 James Knight, Con Cunningham, Judge Cavender, and others
3 James Knight in New Year Edition Leadville Herald Democrat.

Patterson rival candidates for Congress. More than 5000 packed the "Wigwam" to listen to the arguments.[1] After the election this great building was used as a bunk house. The bunks were piled one on top of another clear to the ceiling, and every bunk was sold every night. Not only that but usually a man was allowed but eight hours sleep because somebody else was waiting for the bed. The bunks sold for $1 to $1.50 a night.[2]

Another famous lodging house was conducted by Hiram Hipsley on the S.E. corner of Chestnut and Pine. Hipsley didn't have enough bed clothes to go around; therefore, as fast as a man went to sleep Hipsley would go to his room, secure his bedding and have it ready for the next transient when he arrived. For this privilege Hipsley charged $2 per night and within a few months made enough to retire.[3]

Thousands thronged the streets. In the evening they were crowded from curb to curb with miners, speculators, capitalists, and loungers. Everyone was swept along with the crowd. If one was in a hurry he had to take the middle of the streets. Fossett writing in 1879, says, "Leadville is the livest town the world can show today. It is a marvel of activity. Difficult as it is to make one's way along the main thoroughfares by day, it is still more so just before and after nightfall. Leadville by lamplight fairly 'booms' with excitement and life. The miners then drift into town in swarms, a dozen bands are drumming up audiences for theaters and variety shows; scores of saloons and

....

1, 2, and 3 James M. Knight - Elk's Convention Pamphlet - Confirmed by others.

gambling houses are in full blast, the entire scene gives the town and place the appearance of one grand holiday."[1]

The camp abounded with places of amusement, dance halls, saloons, gambling places, theaters, etc. A number of the theaters and scores of questionable resorts were brilliantly lighted. The performance generally began about ten or eleven o'clock and lasted until day break.[2] "It's day all day in the day time, and no night in Leadville".

The first theater was the old Coleseum on Chestnut opposite the Grand Hotel owned by Search and Caddigan. It was opened with Billy Arlington and Baby Rhinehart as drawing cards. The latter was such a favorite that she had enough money thrown to her to make her rich. This was followed by Woods Opera House the Comique, New Antheneum Vanderville Olympic, Canterbury, Bella Union Grand Central, Little Glove, etc. Colonel Wood had the honor of inflicting upon the people of the camp the first Uncle Tom's Cabin. The leader of all the theaters was the Grand Central. It was built and owned by John Kemp and opened December 9, 1879. The best vaudeville talent in American was shown here for the simple reason that the highest salaries in the country were paid. It was during this period that $1750 was cleared here in one night for the benefit of the sufferers of the Irish famine. The orchestra contained thirty-five pieces. One of the many romances of this old theater was that

....

1 Frank Fossett, - Colorado - Ed. of 1879, P. 415.

2 Hall - Colorado, P. 453.

of Morlachi the premier danseuse with "The Black Crook". She fell in love with Texas Jack the Indian fighter and scout and while here they were married. He died the following year and is buried in Evergreen Cemetery, while she sleeps in a little grave in Maine. This theater was burned in 1885.[1]

Saloons were numerous, extended all the way from Oro City in the gulch to Malta. There probably were in the Carbonate District, not less than 250. Most of these early ones were located on Chestnut and included "The Bank", "Chaplin" and "Gore's Place", "The Delta", "Denver Headquarters", "Forshay", "Harlow, Hirsch, Haughton, Kelley, Lane, Leppel, Little Casino, Little Church, Parlin and Shaw, Padey Rische and McDermith, Pioneer, Pinafore, Remine, Rocky Mountain, Siman, etc., almost without limit. Later they spread to Pine, State, and the Avenue, Most of them did an overtime business. From midnight to sunrise were the busy hours.[2]

Gambling houses were equally numerous. The largest one in the state, operated by C. Hall and Company, located on West Chestnut near the corner of Harrison Avenue, netted an average profit of $32,000 a month. Bill Nye ran another swell place on the same street. Pat Wyman conducted one at the corner of East Second and the Avenue, and across the face of a large clock in black letters were the words, "Don't Swear"! Below the clock on a special made desk was always an open bible. Wyman was the first man to light his building with electricity, and many of

....

1 James M. Knight, Elk's Convention Pamphlet; confirmed by others.

2 Con Cunningham, James M. Knight, James R. McNuce, Julius Edgerton.

the most ignorant thought he was possessed of the devil. He was an eccentric character and before the city was laid out, took up a lot at the intersection of East and West State Street, on which he erected a cabin. When the city was surveyed, the cabin was in the very center of the avenue. The authorities told him to remove the building, which he refused to do, and he held the fort for several days, when the authorities took forcible possession and removed him.[1] "The Texas House" was opened early in April by Harlan and Chaplin of Texas, and was without doubt the swellest gambling house in America. Every room was equipped with a piano, carpets costing three and four dollars a yard, oil paintings worth from $25,000 to $50,000 each, mahogany furniture, etc. On the opening night, the finest dinner ever served in the West was presented to the guests who represented a capital amounting to $75,000,000. Harlan and Chaplin within a few years made a fortune, sold out and returned to Texas.[2] Another famous place bore the legend "Bryon Campbell, light weight champion of the world keeps this saloon. This saloon keeps Bryon Campbell,[3] light weight champion of the world". The storyis told of one gambler who stepped into a place, laid $10,000 on the high card and lost without batting an eye.[4]

....

[1]James M. Knight, Elk's Convention Pamphlet.
[2]James M. Knight, James R. McNeece, Judge Charles Cavender.
[3]Con Cunningham, Ex-Lt.Gov. Breen.
[4]James M. Knight.

The theaters, saloons, gambling houses, together with dance halls, furnished the headquarters for the amusements, the business, the social life and the fights of the entire camp, and were a feature, without which no story or picture of the Rush Days could be complete.

Other places of particular interest included "The Clarendon Hotel" a large frame building erected on the avenue, three squares above Chestnut Street and finished April 10, 1879. The Tabor Opera House, a large brick building just above the Clarendon finished that fall and the Tontine Restaurant. The Clarendon and the Tabor did much to attract the population toward the avenue, and resulted in there being erected there, in less than a year, a long continuous row of more than a mile in length of substantial business structures. The Tabor was at that time the finest Opera House west of Chicago. It was opened November 20, 1879 by J.S. Languiste and Company, who presented the comedy entitled "The Serious Family". The program contained an announcement of a mass meeting to be held in the interest of building a railroad into Leadville; also a statement that there were more than 40,000 people in Leadville and neighboring camps. The Tontine Restaurant was the equal to any in America, and probably the highest priced "grub joint" in the world. Prospectors who stole their claims entertained their friends there, and wine flowed like water.[1]

....

[1]James M. Knight, Julius Edgerton. - History Arkansas Valley, P. 230; - Hall, Vol. II, P. 468.

Great fortunes were made out of mining claims throughout this period. Men who possessed nothing but a grub stake in the morning were rich by night. Prospectors, many of them entirely ignorant of lodes and mining, covered the hills and speculators filled the town. One was ready to snap up every likely looking spot located by the other. Anything in the shape of a hole in the ground could be sold. Capital sought the miner; the miner did not have to seek the capital.[1]

In 1877 A.B.Wood had sold out his entire interest to L.Z. Leiter, a Chicago dry goods man, for but $40,000 and in March 1878 the St. Louis Smelting Company put through the first big transfer of mining property when it bought the Camp Pine, Bird, Keystone and Charleston Claims for $225,000; but after the discovery of the "Little Pittsburgh" only the sky was the limit. Claims changed rapidly and at prices that quickly advanced into the millions.[2] A half interest in one claim was sold one morning for $50,000 and after changing hands several times was repurchased the next day for $225,000.[3] Hundreds of claims were located during the Rush Days; also many a mine was opened up that later proved to be a big producer. "The Little Pittsburgh" which had been producing $8,000 a week was consolidated with the "New Discovery Dives" and Winnemus claims at $20,000,000, and although the mine produced over $4,000,000 in two years, the

....

[1]Judge Cavender - Captain Jenks.
[2]Fossett - Ed. of '79 - P. 411; Hall, P. 434.
[3] James Knight.

company collapsed and carried several others with it. At this time the Iron Mine was brought into litigation and it became necessary to guard the mine with armed men. It had produced $12,000,000 up to this time. Several vain attempts were made to capture it by force. The Chrysolite Company was organized in October 1878 and included the Vulture, Carboniferous, Colorado Chief, and others. The capital stock was $10,000,000. It produced nearly $40,000,000 in one year. The Robert E. Lee located in 1878, soon proved to be the richest mine in the entire district. At the depth of 150 feet, chloride was found that ran 2,000 ounces to the ton. Assays were had showing 80,000 ounces to the ton. Over $4,000,000 was produced in four months. January alone produced better than $300,000, and in a single day $118,500 was produced. When the mine was producing dividends of $90,000 a month, it was suddenly flooded with water. Z. Y. Marshall, its president, discussed draining it several times with Brunton his chief engineer, but could never come to terms, principally because Brunton had a boyish idea that a mine that was worth that much should pay the engineer heavily for draining it. Finally Marshall ordered him to go ahead, then send in his bill. Brunton ordered the biggest pumps that could possibly be used. Now it happened that at this time Mr. Marshall was a candidate for District Judge, and while he absolutely refused to take part in the political scramble, conceived the idea of starting the pumps a few days before the election, and to make this the occasion of a great reception. The pumps were thoroughly tested in advance to prevent mishaps. Everybody in the district, from mine owner to dre driver, was

invited; the office stocked with champagne and cigars for managers and the superintendents, while shaft buildings and ore houses were overflowing with beer and smokes for the miners. Promptly at two o'clock the steam was turned on; the mine whistles began to blow and the tooting was taken up by every whistle on the hill. Both the water and the drinks started flowing at once. The afternoon and evening was long to be remembered as a great success and needless to say Marshall was elected by an overwhelming vote.[1]

Another mine "The Morning Star" purchased by Governor Routt for $10,000, yielded an average of $70,000 per month. The Morning Star Mining Company was organized later with the capital stock of $60,000,000. "The Evening Star" located in 1879 was incorporated modestly for but $500,000 though the mine produced $25,000 a month. The "Matchless" purchased in '79 by Tabor for $117,000 ran at times as high as $100,000 a month. The "A. Y. and Minnie" groups produced better than $2,000,000 in a single year. However, it was not Corman, their locator, who received the benefit of this production, for he had been forced to sell for financial reasons to Graham and Gugenheim. The "Henrietta" located by P.G.Goris, another old time placer miner, was a great producer but Goris too lost out because he was forced to sell when he struck water. The "Silver Cord" "Maid of Erin" "Iron Silver" "Annie" "Catalpa", "Small Hopes" and "Climax" were all good producers at this period.[2]

....

1 and 2 Based upon Hall, Col.; History of Arkansas Valley; Fossett, and local newspaper records; and Leadville and the Gold Belt.

Another entertaining phase of the mining during this period was the claim jumping. Every location was considered a mine and there were many in camp that did not hesitate to jump any spot that looked good. This led to numerous shooting scrapes and affairs of unusual interest.[1]

One of the most famous was the Jim Bush-Arbuckle affair. Bush moved Arbuckle's cabin off of his lot one night at about 12 o'clock and put up one of his own by morning. Immediately there was an argument ending with the shooting of Arbuckle. It cost Bill Bush, owner of the Clarendon, a great amount of money and time to clear his brother of this affair.[2]

Another incident and rather an amusing one was: L.D.Bard built a cabin and one night moved it up on a lot on Harrison Avenue. He told Julius Edgerton, who helped him build the cabin, that he was determined to hold the place with revolvers. Nothing happened during the day, but in the middle of the following night Bard awoke and felt himself being moved off; he rushed out determined to fight, but found himself covered and informed that he was lot jumping and wouldn't be able to get away with it.[3]

Another is told of Rev. Tom Uzzell, the pioneer Methodist Minister. Visiting the site of the first Methodist Church, a lot donated for the purpose, the parson found men unloading lumber upon it. Seeing that they were not disposed to listen

....

[1]Ex.-Lt.Gov. Peter W. Breene - Judge Cavender.
[2]Peter W. Breene - Captain Jenks
[3]Julius Edgerton

to his wordly protest, Tom decided that more strenuous means were necessary. He stripped off his coat. Later Tom said, "I made up my mind if the Lord wanted me to recover that lot, He would give me strength to lick those fellows. And the result showed He was on my side."[1]

Another rather humorous one was that of Mrs. Sarah Ray. She had located some lots early in 1878 on the corner of State and Harrison Avenue, built a slab shanty and put out the sign "Laundry". She did a land office business and with the money later erected a two-story building, but many a time she had to protect her rights from lot jumpers by standing guard all night and the only weapon used was an old broom.[2]

Most lot-jumping affairs were considerably more serious than these last two incidents. The most notorious lot-jumper was Frodsham. He had been born in England, but when seven years old was shipped to Utah by a Morman missionary and trained for the work of the church, but it didn't take and he came to Leadville. He and sixteen followers called the "Black Hillers" seized the north side of west Ninth Street from Harrison Avenue westward, a total of 850 feet.[3]

The numerous cases of lot-jumping and the continual hold-ups, etc., finally aroused the people of the camp, and resulted in Leadville's only lynching. A group of "Vigilantes" formed on

....

1Davis, P. 230-231
2James Knight Elk's Convention Pamphlet.
3History Arkansas Valley, P. 246-250 - James Knight, C.C. Davis, Geo. Boughton. For full account see Hist. Ark. Valley.

the evening of November 19, 1879, and quietly proceeded to the county jail where Frodsham was confined. They compelled under-sheriff Watson to admit them, overpowered the guards, took Frodsham and a young fellow named Stewart from their cells, placed ropes about their neck, took them to an unfinished building where the "Topic Saloon" now stands and swung them from the rafters. In the back of Frodsham's coat was pinned a list of over 50 men who were considered undesirable citizens and were ordered to leave town at once. City Marshall Kelly's name headed the list. The "Undesirables" however, banded together and refused to leave. Steward was only nineteen and protested his innocence to the last. He begged to write a letter to his mother but this they refused. There is much evidence to show that Stewart was innocent, and many old timers are thoroughly convinced of it. However, this affair ended lot-jumping and highway robbery for a time at least.[1]

Mine jumping was also common. The most noted case was that of an attempt by adverse claimants to gain possession of the Iron-Silver Mine, a vast property, with fifty miles of underground works, and millions in dividends. For years Colonel Stocking, a noted "gun man", with an effective force of fifty men, guarded the portals of the mine night and day, while within were mounted several brass cannons. Litigation over this property lasted a decade, and cost hundreds of thousands of dollars.

....

[1]History Arkansas Valley, P. 246-250; James Knight, C.C.Davis, George Boughton. For a full account see Hist. Ark. Valley.

Soon after the case was settled by the Federal Supreme Couft, "Uncle Billy Stevens", principal owner, died. He had become so familiar a figure in the courts, that his friends said he had no desire to live after all cause for litigation was settled.[1]

Mining and gambling were not the only money making business. Great fortunes were made in real estate. The value of town lots increased by jumps. Building sites that could be purchased for $25 in the summer of 1878, sold for several thousand dollars the following winter, and in a single week real estate quadrupled in value.[2] "The Chronicle" had purchased its place upon Harrison Avenue for $175 in the fall of 1878. In January, $8000 was offered for it. Similarly Bush, when he had built the Clarendon had paid $25 a lot for the property and was considered foolish, but in three months the lots were worth $10,000. These are only mere examples. Land anywhere on Chestnut rose to $250 a front foot.[3]

Business was wonderful throughout the Rush Period. Probably 1880 was the big year and according to the statistics gathered by the "Weekly Herald" and published January 8, 1881, there was $15,240,000 worth of merchandise sold in Leadville the previous year, as follows:-

....

1 Davis, P. 233.

2 Fossett, P. 414

3 C.C.Davis; James Knight.

Dry Goods and carpets	900,000
Jewelry, Watches, etc.	175,000
Hardware, tinware, etc.	1,200,000
Machinery	500,000
Clothing	1,000,000
Liquors, Wholesale, Retail, etc.	3,000,000
Cigars and Tobacco	700,000
Gentlemen's Furnishing Goods	150,000
Auctions	200,000
Grocers	2,800,000
Stationers	200,000
Bakeries	250,000
Meat Markets	300,000
Foundries	100,000
Harnesses, Whips, etc.	100,000
Gunsmiths	50,000
Mattress Factory	20,000
Barbers	150,000
Lumber	360,000
Bottling works	60,000
Boots and Shoes	200,000
Furniture	200,000
Crockery	100,000
Gas Fixtures	10,000
Drugs	300,000
Merchant Tailors	75,000
Wood	30,000
Hay and grain	1,500,000
Miscellaneous loan shops	
Pawn Shops, Fruit Shops, etc.	400,000
Undertakers	50,000
Coal	95,000
Total	14,240,000

This did not include hotels, restaurants, etc., which strictly speaking are not dealers in merchandise.

Prices were not particularly high. Sandwiches and cofeee cost but 25¢; soup, crackers, and coffee for 25¢; and first-class meals could be secured for 75¢ and up. With the prosperity of the camp, opportunity for all, and at such prices, there was little excuse for any one going hungry, yet there was a class that preferred begging to working. The story is told of one of these men who made it a habit to wait for the miners as they came off the hill, then ask for what was left in their

buckets. It once happened that the day was very cold, and the miner "dunned for his leavings", genial, replied "Sure you can, but I am afraid they are frozen". "That's all right" answered the loafer. "If you hadn't told me, I wouldn't have known but that that was the way they were cooked."

Clothes and shoes were reasonable, only about 30% higher than Chicago, and about the same as now. Shaves were 50¢ and haircuts 75¢. Whiskey and drinks were 25¢ straight until after the railraod came; then two for a quarter. Cigars were not much higher than now. Nickel ones cost $3.00 a box and Bull Durham 60¢ a pound. Drill steel was 10¢ a pound. Other hardware and mining tools were about a third higher than in Chicago. Feed, owing to the quantity used, was rather high. Oats brought 10¢ a pound, and hay was worth $75 to $100 a ton. Prices dropped after the railroads came in, but even before this, with the exception of the very earliest days of the rush, they were reasonable. Lumber was an exception. It was scarce and in great demand. It had to be hauled in by freight wagons. The demand constantly exceeded the supply, one firm selling over a million feet and never had a stick on hand. Everything was contracted for before and driven direct to its destination. Those who were building, in their impatience, fell into the habit of going down the road to meet the lumber wagons; overbidding the purchaser, and bringing it in. Therefore, it became customary for those who had contracted for the material, to meet it on the road, and with a

revolver in each hand, bring in the lumber.[1]

The Kansas Pacific Railroad put out in 1879 a guide to Leadville, in which they declared that every branch of business is represented in Leadville. There were then within the city ten hay and grain stores, ten lumber yards, twelve blacksmith shops, four banks, over twenty hotels, eight smelting works, twelve dry goods stores, eight hardware stores, eight clothing stores, thirty groceries, thirteen boot and shoe shops, fifteen livery stables, twenty-five bakeries, fourteen sawmills, twenty meat markets, seven drug stores, fifteen jewelers, seven furniture stores, twenty-five cigar stands, and thirty-eight restaurants.[2]

The rents were high. Eligible building lots on Harrison Avenue and Chestnut Street ranged from$1,000 to $8,000, which six months before could have been bought from $50 to $100. A good store 25 x 40 rented for $200 to $300. Offices rented from $30 to $100 per month. Board in private families cost from $7 to $15 per week, single meals in the restaurants from 25¢ upward; a man could live in Leadville as cheaply as anywhere, as shown by the following prices:

Heavy flannel shirts, 75¢ to $1.00; flannel drawers, 75¢ to $1.00; flannel underwear, $3 to $3.50 per suit; overalls, $1 to $1.25; overall coats, $2, $3, and $3.50; all wool cassimere suits $15 to $18; blankets $3 to $3.50; rubber boots, knee, $3.50;

....

1 George Boughton & Con Cunningham, Peter W. Breene.
2 An 1879 Guide to Leadville, P. 7-8.

hip, $4.50; overshoes, $2; shoes, nailed, $1.75 to $2; Sugar, 6½ pounds for $1.; Java, 40¢; Ham, 16¢; Bacon, 13¢; Eggs 40¢ per dozen; Butter 35¢ to 45¢; Flour $7 per cwt.; Potatoes 5½¢ a pound.[1]

The merchant, lumberman, mechanic and professional man had all the business they could possibly do. One advocation helped another and all helped the freighter. The freight business done between Leadville and the railraod was something amazing. The nearest railroad station was at Canon City, and the traffic from that place, or from Colorado Springs to the Carbonate Camp literally covered the raod. Horses, mules, bull teams, everything that pulled, was used to haul freight to Leadville. There were three freight lines and between five and seven thousand men engaged in it. The Colorado Springs freight line alone had 2000 animals engaged in the service and yet lacked men and mules to such a degree as to be practically blockaded throughout the entire winter and spring of 1879. There was from six to fourteen mules on a wagon and one trailer; the usual number, however, was eight mules to two wagons, with but one driver who sat on a saddled mule; i.e., the mule nearest the wagon on the left side, and drove with a jerk line. Clothing, liquor, lumber, and lots of coke (used in smelting) were hauled in.[2]

....

[1] An 1879 Guide to Leadville, P. 7-8.
[2] Fossett, P. 414, and C.J.Deane.

The round trip from Leadville to Colorado Springs took fifteen days. In February 1880 the South Park Railroad practically reached Buena Vista, and that became the freighting point for the local camp.[1]

One novel feature during this period was the great number of charcoal kilms scattered about. The region was then heavy with timber and charcoal was in great demand for the smelters. As the supply of timbers were rapidly exhausted the remains of the kilms have almost completely disappeared.[2]

Probably one of the most exciting phases of the "Rush Period" was the great number of hold-ups, murders, and gun fights. Everybody went armed, many in camp were professional gun men; others drank to excess and fought; some got excited and shot; while there were still others who like a grey painted war ship roved the seas in search of trouble. It was these various classes and peculiar conditions of the local camp that made the killing so frequent. Probably the first murder was commited April 25, when James Bloodsworth shot and killed City Marshall George O'Connor in Bill Nye's gambling parlor. Bloodsworth, known as "Tex", ran from Leadville to Malta; here he stole the horse of County Sheriff Tucker and made his escape and has never been captured.[3]

Another well-known shooting scrap was that of Mart Duggan and Lamb. They had a big argument on the corner of Fifth and

....

1 James Knight.
2 C. Hearsey; - Con Cunningham
3 James Knight; James McNeece; Judge Cavender.

Pine. Lamb pulled his gun, but Duggan shot first. Later he was acquitted by the coroner's jury presided over by Coroner Law.[1]

There was a tough character by the name of Brocky who was in love with a barmaid at the Red Light Saloon, and becoming jealous threatened to shoot his rival on sight. The rival went out, obtained a gun, came back and fired five shots at Brocky everyone of which went through his heart. After they picked Brockey up and had him laid out, he was asked if there was anything they could do for him. "Sure, get me a coffin" was the reply. The murderer was acquitted.[2]

Frank Richard, another gambler, cleaned a fellow from Missouri out of everything and then refused him the price of a meal, whereupon the Missourian drilled him full of holes.

Bill Ballad, shift boss at the Chrysolite, had an argument and was shot by his brother-in-law.[3]

During an election gun fight, a man named Long Spencer stuck his head out of the Pioneer saloon and had his nose shot off.[4]

In a saloon fight one night on State Street, about 50 shots were fired and the bartender was killed but no bullet could be found. Later it was discovered it had entered his mouth and lodged in his brain.[5]

....

[1]Carbonate Weekly Chronicle - Jan 1, 1881, P.4.
2 George Boughton
3 James McNeece
4 James McNeece
5 George Boughton

In the summer of 1880 a noted affair occurred in the store owned by Manville and McCarthy, leading hardware and miners' supply store. Charles Blakewell, a miner employed by them, came to the store to collect his wages. A big dispute followed and they got rather noisy. When Policeman John Carville entered Bakewell told him to stop, but he advanced. Bakewell pulled his gun and shot him through the heart; then fled by the back door pursued by Officer Stewart who fired repeatedly, but missed. At the corner of Third and Pine, Bakewell turned and shot Officer J.G.Stewart. He was arrested later and tried and sentenced to life imprisonment, but pardoned in 1892 by Governor Routt.[1]

Johnnie Keeper, one of the cleverest card dealers in the camp, was shot by four men who claimed he was crooked.[2]

Earl of Kentucky shot Sam Townsend on Harrison Avenue. They had hardly spoken when the shot was fired.[3]

Another affair was that of two prospecters from Tennessee Pass who met on Chestnut Street; one drew a revolver, the other swung a rifle; two shots and both dropped dead. The cause of the trouble was never known.[4]

Alexander was shot March 15 in his own dance hall by McCarthy. The latter was drunk, and the former tried to put him out, when McCarthy pulled his gun and killed him.[5] On April 11,

....

1 Carbonate Weekly Chronicle, Jan. 1, 1881, P.4

2, 3, and 4 James McNeece, Confirmed by others.

5 Carbonate Weekly Chronicle, Jan. 1, 1881, P.4

Lawrence Fitzgerald was shot dead by George Tattersall. This was a case of lot-jumping, and at the time the murder occurred, public feeling ran high and lynching was suggested.[1]

Two days later John Curley was killed by the notorious bravo Ed Burns, who immediately left the camp without being pursued. He is believed to have killed several persons before.[2]

The same day J. W. Overman shot Thomas Nugent in one of the variety theaters.[3]

On June 19, Rosencrantz, who claimed he found John Langmeyer in the act of robbing his cabin, shot him dead.[4]

Three weeks later we find that Edward Dillian was murdered by William Clark. A woman was at the bottom of this dispute.[5]

Another time a man robbed a prospector's cabin in the hill. The owner tracked the thief to East Third Street. Both fired at the same time and both fell dead, shot through the heart. Again"Two dead shots" had met.[6]

Then there was a shooting affair between John C. Blake and his wife in the Little Pittsburgh saloon. John said she was not his wife. She pulled a revolver but missed.[7]

In July 1881, Francis Gilburt, Minick, and Rosencrantz were hung for the murder of John Langmeyer, and James McCullen the previous year.[8]

....

1, 2, 3, and 4
Carbonate Weekly Chronicle, Jan. 1881, P.4.

5 Carbonate Weekly Chronicle, Jan. 1881, P.4

6 Leadville and the Gold Belt, P. 111

7 James McNeece, confirmed by others.

8 Judge Cavender

These are only a very few of the murders and shooting scrapes of the Rush Days. Dozens and dozens more were killed. The papers of that time are full of them, and there is scarcely a corner in Leadville upon which a man has not been killed. However, little attention was paid to them because such lawlessness was so common and from a standpoint of public interest either then or now, they did not amount to much.

The town was also full of notorious crooks. Probably all the bandits of the southwest were there in the winter of 1879. It is certain that Jesse James was there and interested in mining property; also the Younger Brothers, Doc. Holiday, Haregan Bill and his band of Wyoming toughs were among the wide-awake citizens of the Cloud City.[1]

Deaths through this period were very numerous. Because of lack of accommodations a great many died from exposure. In 1880, 300 died from pneumonia and this fact has given Leadville a reputation for pneumonia which it does not deserve. Excellent medical authorities insist that pneumonia is no more serious in Leadville than elsewhere. These deaths were due to lack of shelter, the life the people led, etc., and not to altitude. In 1880, 850 died, but at that the death rate was less than that of Denver for the same year.[2] We have read and heard

....

1 James Knight - Captain Jenks

2 Dr. A. J. McDonald - James Knight.

stories that men died so fast in the carbonate camp that it was impossible to bury them and that they worked three shifts at the grave yard and used the same coffin over and over again, but these stories are pure exaggerations.

The Rush Days were magnificent, wonderful, and strenuous and well deserve a place in history, but there are phases that have grown more strenuous by stories wrought by time and of that kind of stories, those in regard to the number and treatment of the dead are probably the most groundless.

CHAPTER IV

LEADERS AND CHARACTERS OF THE RUSH DAYS

The most important men in Leadville during the Rush Days were men suddenly made prominent by the new mines. These men immediately arose to positions of great influence, politically and financially. The most important, and the best example of this class was Horace A. W. Tabor. We have already told of Tabor's early history, his coming to the Gulch, his store, and the discovery of the "Little Pittsburgh". This discovery immediately made him the big financial and political power of the camp. He was the leader in organizing the city; he served as its first mayor; he brought form and order out of rudimentary chaos; he organized its police force, the Bank of Leadville, the gas company, and the fire department. To the latter, the Tabor Hose Company, he presented a $1,200 carriage and 1,250 feet of hose. Tabor also spent $10,000 equipping the Tabor Light Cavalry, a body of fifty men. In 1881 he held large interests in many rich mines as follows: The Matchless, Scooper, Dunkin, Chrysolite, Union, Emma, Denver City, Henrietta, Maid of Erin, Empire, Hibernia, and May Queen. Besides his great building activity in Leadville, we soon find him carrying his schemes to Denver. He erected there the Windsor Hotel, which surpassed anything yet seen west of the Missouri. And the Tabor Opera House at Denver cost fully $200,000. He also owned 890 of the 2,000 shares in the First National Bank of Denver. In 1878 he was elected Lieutenant-Governor, and when Henry M. Teller became a member of the cabinet, Tabor was elected to fill out his un-

expired term as U.S. Senator. He was a candidate for re-election but lost to Judge Bowen, by a majority of one vote. Later he was chairman of the Republican State Central Committee, President of the Denver Chamber of Commerce and Board of Trade. Before his death Tabor's luck turned and he lost his great fortune. In 1898 he was glad to accept the Postmastership of Denver. And C. C. Davis writes that he has seen a man once worth ten million and who sat in the United States Senate, pushing slag at $3.00 per day.[1]

Another great leader was "Uncle Billy" Stevens. We have already told of his coming to the camp and the great part he played in the development of the Carbonates. He took an active interest in all things pertaining to the camp, and was a popular leader.

Joseph H. Wells, born in England 1842, came to America at eleven, to Kansas in '54, and to California Gulch in the fall of 1860. He served in the Civil War, returned to Colorado in 1866 and engaged in placer maning. Later he held an interest in several mines, and served as Chairman of the Republican Central Committee for four years. He was also elected Clerk and Recorder of Lake County in 1875,'77, and '79.[2]

Judge A. S. Weston also came to the Gulch in 1860 arriving July 14. He spent eleven years placer mining; then started a

....

[1]History of Arkansas Valley, P.378-384; Judge Cavender - and Daivs, P. 318

[2]History of Arkansas Valley, P. 387.

ranch, and for years was the only practicing attorney in Lake County. Later he was elected State Senator.[1]

G. W. Quimble, Cashier of the Miners Exchange Bank, came to Leadville in April 1860. He was also Treasurer for the Highland Chief and Glass Pendery Mines.[2]

Thomas R. Agnew arrived from New York City in 1877. He was wealthy, and did a great deal to interest Eastern capital in Leadville mining properties.[3]

Charles C. Baldwin, graduate of the University of Michigan, in 1875, came to California Gulch in 1877; was an engineer at the Iron Silver, Robert E. Lee, and other mines. He made the first map of Leadville and vicinity, showing about 800 mines. He laid out many of the principal streets of Leadville.[4]

Charles Boettcher came to Leadville in 1879; had a hardware and mining supply store, with a stock estimated at $100,000.[5]

Tom Walsh, one time owner of the Camp Bird, and proprietor during the Rush Days of the Grand Hotel, the pioneer hostlery in Leadville, was also widely known. He was a large-hearted, genial, sympathic, bluff fellow. He later became a multimillionaire and won fame as the distinguished mining partner of King Leopold of Belgium and the lavish entertainer of official Washington.[6]

....

[1]History of Arkansas Valley, P. 386-387.
[2]History of Arkansas Valley, P. 384.
[3]Ibid, P. 309
[4]Ibid, P. 313
[5]Ibid, P. 315
[6]Davis, P. 113.

John McCombe, born 1851 in Ireland, came to Leadville, April 1877, located the Maid of Erin, Crescent, Evening Star, the Little Darling, Big Chief, Little Champion, Monte Christo, and others. Also owned at one time a third interest in the Little Pittsburgh; He served as alderman in Leadville and was a canddidate for Lieutenant-Governorm. Davis writes he once went back to Ireland and gave a present to every one in town.[1]

Other leading mining men included Billy Borden, associated with Tabor in the Chrysolite; George Hook and his partner August Rische, although originally only Pittsburgh shoemakers, held a prominent place after its discovery and development of the "Little Pittsburgh". Others include George Fryer, who located the New Discovery, etc., and after whom the hill was named; the Gallagher Brothers, locators of the Camp Bird; George Robinson, owner of the Robinson, later elected Lieutenant-Governor; Isaacs Kueffer, A. R. Meyers, etc.

Rische retired from the ownership of the Little Pittsburgh with $310,000.[2]

J. G. Marshall came to Leadville in '78. He was President of the Robert E. Lee, which made its owners rich.[3]

J. J. DuBois came to the Gulch in '77. In December he located in snow waist deep the "Little Eaton". It afterwards sold for $1,200,000. He was elected mayor in 1884.[4]

....

[1]History Arkansas Valley, P. 356.
2, 3, 4.
Bancroft, Volume 28, P. 507.

Peter Finerty came in early, purchased the Little Chief, took out $300,000, and sold for $350,000.[1]

Luther M. Goddard started practicing law in Leadville in 1879, made $200,000 out of the Pendery Mine.[2]

Peter W. Breene located in the Gulch in '74, became part owner of the Crown Point, Pinnacle, and Big Chief. He was elected Lieutenant-Governor in 1884.[3]

J. B. Grant came to Leadville in '78 and started the smelting works of the J.B.Grant & Company. They did a monthly[4] business of over half a million dollars.

George L. Henderson was first Postmaster.[5]

F. D. Mainville and W.H.Brisbane came in '79, invested what capital they could command in mining property and in '82 erected the Mainville Block at a cost of $40,000. They held a large amount of other Leadville real estate.[6]

Among the leaders might also be mentioned Charles Vivian, an actor by profession and at one time the dramatic critic on The Chronicle. His work was pleasing. Later he conceived the idea of a great secret society - The Benevolent Protective Order of Elks. He wrote the manual for it and organized the first lodge.[7] He died at 133 East Fourth Street, March 20, 1880. Funeral services were held in The Tabor Opera House - now the Elks Opera House, but a decade later his remains were

....

[1]History Arkansas Valley, P. 333.
2 and 3
Bancroft, Volume 28, P. 508
[4]History Arkansas Valley, P. 336
[5]History Arkansas Valley, P. 340
[6]Bancroft, Volume 28, P. 528.
[7]C. C. Davis, P. 176

removed from Leadville by the Elks to "Elks' Rest", Mt. Hope Cemetary, Boston. The Chronicle wrote "Vivian, the generous, Vivian, the talented, Vivian, the only Vivian is no more"[1]

One of the sights of the town in this period was a team of Elks named Nan and Pete driven by the Hon. "Con" Cunningham, then Mayor of Malta. Cunningham had come to the Gulch early in 1874 and went to work onStarr's placer. Later he moved to Malta and ran a saloon.[2]

Malta was at this time quite a place. It had been started with the erection of the smelter in 1875 and by 1880 it had a number of saloons, a group of fine stores, a hotel, and about 1300 voters. "Con" was mayor several times and a prominent leader. He was one of the few that opposed the attempt to make Malta the railroad metropolis of the West. Malta was incorporated at this time and as its incorporation has never been revoked by the State Legislature, it is probably one of the smallest incorporated cities in the world today. This team of Elks attracted a good deal of attention and Con received an offer of $4,000 for them from a Denver merchant, but he absolutely refused to part with them. Cunningham claims he drove them from Leadville to Fairplay repeatedly; that one time he left Malta at 9 o'clock, spent an hour and a half in Fairplay, and returned by 5:30. When we remarked that this was "going some", he solemnly assured us

....

[1]Elks Convention Pamphlet - Leadville, June 1907.

[2]Con Cunningham supplied a great deal of valuable information for this history; also spent much time and effort helping me to locate ~~some~~ material, etc. He died very shortly after he gave me the last of it.

that those folks "did go some" and there is plenty of evidence to substantiate his statements.[1]

Besides the prominent leaders, there were also a number of unique characters, known by everyone in the local camp. One of the most conspicious of these was "Broken Nose Scotty" (his real name was James Ellis). Scotty was an excellent prospector, located the Highland Chief, the Highland Mary and several others that were paying claims. However, Scotty frequently drank to excess, and on one occasion in November 1879, he was arrested for being drunk and was taken to jail. As Scotty did not have sufficient coin of the realm to pay his fine, he was set to work on the chain gang. A few days later a gentlemen arrived at the jail and asked for James Ellis, but the Jailer said he had no one by that name. However, when informed that the man had a broken nose, he immediately produced Scotty. The stranger asked, "You have a claim on "Carbonate Hill,"

"Yes, Sir"

"How much will you take for it?"

"$30,000."

"Come with me to my lawyers, make out the papers, and the money is yours".

Scotty explained the Jailer was so fond of him that he couldn't hope to get away unless some one paid his fine. The

....

[1]Con Cunningham. - Peter W. Breene.

stranger paid the money and the two went out together. Next morning when the bank opened Scotty was on hand to draw his $30,000. He immediately went to the jail, paid the fine of every inmate, took them up and bought each a complete new outfit of clothes, from shoes to hat, then took them to the Tontine Restaurant and ordered the best meal the house could set up. Before midnight everyone including Scotty was back in jail. A few weeks later he left for Scotland to visit his old mother, who lived in the little Scottish town made famous as the birthplace of Harry Lauder.[1]

Scotty bought her a home and made liberal provisions for life for her. Not long after he reappeared in Leadville, busted again as usual; however, he got a grub stake and was off for the hills and before the end of the year, had sold several claims at good figures. Scotty had a pardner named Tom Durkam. He was an ex-prize fighter and also had a broken nose and was without doubt one of the funniest men that ever struck the camp. One time after Scotty had disposed of a claim at a good figure, he was treating all his friends lavishly at the Tontine. He gladly bought Tom anything he wanted, but Tom wasn't satisfied; he wanted to set up the treats too; hence asked Scotty for money. Scotty said, "Nope, ye don't know how to handle money, but I'll buy ye anything ye want".[2]

....

[1]James M. Knight, Elks Convention Pamphlet
[2]James McNeece

Another character known by all was John Morrissey. Diamond Joe Reynolds who owned "The Diamond Joe" steamship line on the Mississippi River sent Morrissey to Leadville in the early days of the camp to see what he could locate for him. Morrissey was ignorant of mining and soon bought a salted claim for $10,000. After sinking the shaft thirty more feet, however, ore was struck, and the mine, the Crown Point, produced about $3,000,000. This greatly added to Joe Reynold's fortune and made Morrissey rich. Morrissey immediately became a prominent character about the camp, and many an excellent story is told in regard to him, some of these probably without foundation. One of the most common of these stories is that Morrissey carried a beautiful $500 timepiece and as it was a well-known fact that he couldn't tell time his friends would say, "John, what time is it by your watch"? Morrissey would produce his watch and say, "Look for yourselves, and then ye'll know I ain't lying to ye".[1]

Another entertaining story told of John Morrissey was when asked to contribute towards the purchase of a chandelier for the Catholic church, said, "Sure and I'll help ye out, but I don't believe a d--- one of ye can play it when ye do get it"

C. C. Davis writes Morrissey made a sight draft on the Treasurer of the United States for the price of a plot of ground sold to the Government for a fish hatchery, not being satisifed with the slow method of auditing claims by the Representative of Uncle Sam.[2]

....

[1]James Knight, James McNeece - also confirmed by others.
[2]C. C. Davis, P. 318.

Again it is told that on a trip to Denver he noticed a sign "Keep off the grass" in one of the parks. John studied it a moment, then backed up with a startled "Smallpox by gosh"[1]

On observing a gentlemen eating celery at one of the swell hotels in Denver, Morrissey remarked to his pardner "Look at that son-of-gun eating the bouquet".[2]

However, Morrissey was a long ways from being a fool in some respects. One time a fellow tried to get him to endorse a check, told Morrissey it wouldn't cost him a thing, and if he would only sign it, he could collect his money. Morrissey said, "Who'll give ye the money if I sign that thing"?

"Why, Mr. Hunter will".

"All right", said Morrissey, "Ye get Mister Hunter to sign it for ye, and I'll give ye the money".[3]

Patty McNanar was Morrissey's right-hand man. He was one of the fanciest dressers, and foulest speaking fellows in camp. One day Healey,Morrissey's superintendent at the Crown Point, sent Patty with a note to Morrissey for supplies. Morrissey pretended to look at it carefully, and then said very solemnly, "Patty if Healey fired ye, I can't help ye". Patty, however, explained; then John told him to get whatever supplies he wanted and in the future to go to h---- with his notes.[4]

....

1, 2, and 3
James Knight, James McNeece - also confirmed by others.

4 Knight and McNeece. These stories are frequently repeated; however, Brancroft, Volume 25, P. 508, lists Morrissey as one of Colorado's "millionaires".

Morfissey was a tall dark fellow, over six feet, and looked fine on a horse. He was very fond of horses, and he owned at one time the best string in the West. He toured the East with them, and it was here that he lost his money in gambling, frauds, etc. Later he returned to Leadville without a cent, and finally died in the poorhouse.[1]

Jack McComb already mentioned as a leader staged several unique affairs. The most interesting one was as follows: Jack had made a big sale to Tabor and was having a good time at the Grand, setting them up freely to all comers. During the evening a fellow named Travers who had a big reputation as a rough and tumble fighter and as a gun man, came in to the Grand. McComb bought him the drinks, told him that he (McComb) was a mighty good man too, and would like to convince him. The doors were closed, and the fight was staged to a finish. Jack won the fight from this Nevada terror, but both were nearly dead. After it was over McComb took care of him, paid all of his doctor bills, etc.[2]

Another unusual character was Jack Shedding, locator of the Robinson and other mines. He was the cleverest prospector in the camp and never worked at an unsuccessful mine. He made a dozen stakes, but went through them all. His practice was about as follows: He would go out in the hills, work until he struck a good claim, return to Leadville, sell it proceed

....

[1]Knight and McNeece. These stories are frequently repeated; however, Bancroft, Vol. 25, P. 508, lists Morrissey as one of Colorado's "millionaires.

[2]James McNeece.

to spend the money, then return to the hills and repeat the process.[1]

Andre Christol, the great wrestler, although in camp only a short time, made a great reputation by trying to clean out State street one Sunday afternoon, and although he was a hercules in strength he failed on this self-appointed task; however, it took the united efforts of six policemen, a team of horses, and an express wagon to land him in the bastile at the foot of Pine street.[2]

"Chicken Bill" was another character with a reputation. His real name was William Lovell, and he received his decoration after he had been caught on the road in a severe snow storm with a load of chickens. A week after the storm a party was sent out to search for him and found him in a sheltered spot, quietly living off of his load of chickens. Bill visited all of the Colorado camps practically and had a great reputation as a mine salter. It was he who sold Tabor the Chrysolite, and it is also claimed that he was the first one to use a shot gun to shoot gold dust into quarts, and there is no doubt that he was an authority on every know form of mine salting.[3]

An interesting old timer that is still here is Captain Jenks. He had a lot in 1879 where the post office now stands, but very soon moved to his present claim at the top of Carbonate Hill. Here he has worked away on the same claim all these years.

....

1 James McNeece
2 John R. Curly - Elks Convention Pamphlet
3 A. Y. Corman- James Knight.

At three different times Tabor advanced him money to enable him to keep up the work, and after Tabor was unable to aid him financially himself, he secured Chicago parties to put up money for Jenks to continue work. The claim is a likely looking spot, is down 600 feet, and Jenks has been expecting to "strike it" every summer, but so far without luck; however, we heartly agreed with Tabor when he said, "Jenks, I hope you strike a million; you sure deserve it; you're the best sticker I ever saw".[1]

John R. Curly, police magistrate in Leadville in 1880, tells an interesting story of one of the early politicians, Alderman Jennings. In the early days of his judicial career he was approached by this alderman, who informed him that one of his constituents was in jail for over indulging in liquor, and asked what he proposed to do about it. Duly impressed with the dignity of his office, Mr. Curly announced with a magisterial air and with great dignity, that when the prisoner was brought before him for trial, he would receive even and exact justice. "Justice" shrieked the thoroughly aroused and irate alderman, "For heaven's sake give him anything but justice; if the man had justice he would have been in the Canon City Penitentiary long ago".[2]

Soapy Smith, the great confidence man, was well known in camp. He pulled a number of tricks and succeeded in selling

....

[1]Captain Jenks gave me this data himself. And the morning after I wrote the above paragraph back in the spring of 1916, he died. The claim is now owned and worked by his son.

[2]John R. Curly, Elks Convention Pamphlet

gold bricks to numerous easterners. Soapy was killed in the gold rush in Alaska.[1]

The Reverend Thomas A. Uzzell was a well-known character. He came here in February 1878 and erected the first Protestant Church. Now Leadville in 1878 was not exactly an encouraging place for religious endeavor; however, "Parson Tom" as the boys called him, was just the right man to do his Father's work in the local camp. He solicited the money for his church and religious works in the saloons himself; married a couple in a well-known den, and in fact, did sincerely the customary religious work under the conditions that prevailed in the local camp. He was loved and respected by all. The story is told that one time in one of the well-know saloons, he was accosted by a drunken teamster who asked him to drink, and when he politely refused, the man insisted and tried to make him. Another miner pulled a gun and ordered the drunken teamster to either respect the parson or have his brains blown out, and to take his choice quickly. People usually had to take their choise quickly in the days when Leadville was in its glory.[2] There was considerable difference between Uzzell and De Witt Talmadge, the eminent Brooklyn devine who later took Breecher's place. He visited Leadville in 1880 and asked to be shown the town. They took him through the worst parts, the toughest saloons, the noisiest gambling houses, and the lowest dives, described the worst of the shootings, robberies, etc., and when the Reverend

....

1 and 2
James Knight.

returned to Brooklyn he wrote his impression of the West and said "Leadville was a second edition of H---".[1]

Orth Stern was one of the most unusual absurdities that ever struck the camp. He was a remarkable reporter, had a mind as active as the fan of an aeroplane and as clear as the tone of a bell, a clear lucid style. He started his brilliant work on the Chronicle by a hot exposure of the Leadville doctors. He showed but few of the hundred alleged doctors were entitled to practice. Later he urged a scheme on the local sheriff to jerk the heads off of prisoners, and before and after being in Leadville he was a criminal with a large and varied, and vicious record.[2]

Another unique writer was Colonel Joyce, also of the Chronicle. He wrote splendid editorials. Later, however, he returned to the use of liquor and wrote silly poems entitled, "An Apostrophe to the Moon", "Lines on a Stage Horse", "The Red-Eyed Blue-Haired Biscuit Shover of the Vendome," etc. This falling from grace, lost him his place on the Chronicle

After his death in Washington City, in March 1915, was found the following:

> "To my daughters, Libbie and Florence
> In equal proportions to share
> I give all cash and property
> When my spirit is soaring in the air.
>
> "And appoint Mrs. James J. Lampton
> To execute this my last will
> When I rest 'neath the blooming flowers,
> In lot 444 on Oak Hill".[3]

....

[1] This is a Jim Knight's story

[2] Davis, P. 159-166

[3] Davis, P. 173-174

Mike Costello was another character famed for his quick native wit and cleverness at repartee. Delegate to a Democratic County Convention, the proceedings of which had not been at all to his liking -- all of his friends having been defeated in their ambition for representation on the ticket nominated -- Mike started the body with:

"Mr. Chairman: I rise to a pint of order".

The Chair:"The Gentlemen will state his point of order"

Mr.Costello: "I'll bet yez tin dollars the ticket is downed".

And it was.[1]

Notwithstanding there was a Democratic newspaper being published in Leadville at the time, deserving and entitled to the Party's patronage, Mike always saw to it that the committee's needs in the printing line were supplied by Davis and the Chronicle. This resulted in his extraordinary party disloyalty being called in question by the committee, and Mike made an elaborate speech ending with:

"And, gentlemen, I want to tell yez that whin it's Dimocracy to go back on Davis, I'm no longer a Dimocrat".[2]

Another character of the camp, known far and wide for his geniality and good-heartedness was Bill De Vere, "The Tramp Poet of the West", who ground out verses, of a crude yet ever cheerful descriptive character, with the utmost facility. Thus, over a State Street bar, did he immortalize a mining camp tributary to Leadville, named "Ten Mile", for no

....
1 and 2
Davis, P. 319

better reason than that it was that distance from nowhere.

The shades of eve were falling fast
As up through Leadville Village passed,
A "Mick" who bore through mud and ice
A hickory shirt, with this device:
"Ten Mile or bust".

His hat was slouched, he'd one cock eye,
That piped off every passer-by;
The boot-black shouted, "Have a shine?"
The Mick replied, "I'll hunt a mine!"
Ten mile or bust!"

"Beware the pine tree's withered branch,
Beware a 'dead fall' called Chalk Ranch",
Was Hoodoo Brown's last good night;
The Mick replied far up the height,
"Ten Mile or bust."

The dance hall girl said, "Stay and try
A little glass of dance hall rye;
I'll be your darling, dear Gazelle",
The Mick replied, "Oh, go to ------ well,
"Ten Mile or bust."

Next morning, as the Ten Mile stage
Was going up the narrow gauge,
A hickory shirt hung on a rail,
With these words printed on the tail,
"Ten Mile or bust".[1]

Professor Ives, a graduate of Oxford University, England, a fluent conversationalist in Latin and Greek, a finished violinist, was another strange character who when in his cups amused the patrons of the different resorts with selections from the great masters. He would also amuse them with stories of mythical history. He died in a saloon at Stringtown in 1880.[2]

Colonel Grahame, partner of Tom Scott, the railroad magnate of America, and whose check at one time was good for half a million, came to Leadville in the early days. He was an

....

[1]Davis, Pl 320-321

[2]James Knight - Elk's Convention Pamphlet

odd character and later died in the county poorhouse.[1]

Howard Clarke went about with a pocket full of cigars and would button hole anyone whom he could get to listen; then tell them about the valuable claims that he had located. He would give his victims cigars freely and this was the only inducement to listen to him. After they had listened as long as they felt their duty, they would disappear, and Clarke would be forced to find a new victim.[2]

Louis Bryan was an old army officer, and would keep the company spell-bound for hours while he recorded reminiscences of the Civil War. Though the poor fellow was as crazy as a bat, due to a scalp wound, yet a great many thoroughly enjoyed his stories, and everybody liked him.[3]

"Crazy Jane" was another oddity. She gathered the laundry from various saloons, and although her work was satisfactory, she never missed an opportunity to tell that her husband was a pirate, and had stolen her from her parents when she was a beautiful young girl. Later, according to Jane's story, her husband was hung at the yard-arm of a battle ship, and upon receiving the news she drifted West and landed in the Carbonate Camp.[4]

The "Duck" was another demented washwoman. She was called this from the way she want about the streets waving her arms up and down.[5]

....

1, 2, and 3 James Knight - all these stories told by James M. Knight were published from time to time in the Herald Democrat during the long period Mr. Knight was associated with that paper. Some were secured from the files, but most of them were repeated by him for use in this account.

4 James Knight - Elks Convention Pamphlet

5 James Knight.

Another unique and well-known character was a man named Wanen, a broken down actor, He was always to be found on Chestnut Street, and glad of the chance to spout Shakespeare by the hour. And because of this, he received the nickname of "Hamlet's Father".[1]

Another oddity was "Old Pop" Wyman. We have already mentioned his gambling house, with its open bible and painted injunction across the clock "Don't Swear", but in addition to his gambling house Pop ran a variety theatre. And here he showed his ingenuity and originality by his style of advertising. Instead of calling attention to the great array of talent to be seen nightly in his place, he ridiculed his house, the company, the music, etc. He got out a small dodger in bold black type as follows:[2]

Old Pop's Old Theatre

No One Goes Near it Now Since Other Houses are Open

No Success for Our Company. They Don't get Their Salary and None but Hams Work there.

No Bill of Any Account This Week. Nothing - New. Pap Could Not Get the People; in fact Boys, Pap is getting Sick - Stay Away. Don't Go Near the Old Fellow

No Good Music

Only a One-Horse Show; Stay Away, and You'll be Satisfied. Next Week Will Be Worse, if possible, Than this Week for Old Pap is Drinking.

....

1 and 2 James Knight.

This, of course, was completely different than the usual run of advertising; however, people caught on and the house was crowded every night.[1]

There were other unique characters, but those whom we have described were the best known and the most picturesque.

....

1 James Knight.

CHAPTER V

GROWTH OF LEADVILLE

We have already told that Leadville in the spring of 1877. consisted of a handful of log houses scattered along California Gulch, below the Harrison Smelter and appropriately called Slab Town; also how in June, Charles Mater started the first store and how this was followed by others.

The beginning of the new year 1878 found the settlement without a name and without an organization. A petition had been drawn asking for a post office; this necessitated the adoption of a name; hence on the fourteenth of January, eighteen citizens in response to a call, met in a little wagon shop on the present corner of Pine and Chestnut Streets to take the preliminary steps for a town organization. There was a great discussion over a name. "Harrison", "Myers", "Agassiz", "Cerussite" "Carbonate", "Lead City". were suggested, discussed, objected to, and finally Leadville proposed by C. Cramer and agreed upon. There are many stories of this meeting, varying in details, but the story as written here seems to be the most authentic. Governor Routt, by proclamation, called the first city election to be held January 26. H.A.W. Tabor was elected Mayor and C. E. Anderson, Clerk. At the regular election in April, succeeding, Mr. Tabor was reelected and J.C.Cramer was chosen clerk.[1]

Then in May, as we have already told, was discovered the "Little Pittsburgh" and this produced the Rush. Within a few

....

[1] This story is compounded from many varying authorities, but as told here seems to be the most accurate. See Hall, Vol.II, P. 446.

months Leadville had grown to such an extent that a transformation into a city of the second class was justified. W.H.James was elected Mayor and John W. Zollers, City Treasurer. M.J.Murphy, E.C.Kavanaugh, John McComb, Samuel McMillen, P.J. Kelly, and John D. Monroe were the aldermen.[1]

The reader is already familiar with the events of the Rush Days, the crowds, the rapid building up of the city, the tremendous excitement, etc., as recited in a previous chapter, but there yet remains the necessity of a brief discussion of the coming of the railroads, the founding of its banks, the erecting of its churches, the growth of its schools, the history of its press, post office, smelters,police department, fire department, etc.

When Leadville first began to assume the character and proportions of a city, it was a long ways from a railroad. The nearest point was Canon City, 122 miles away.[2] The Denver and South Park had years before been projected to be built up the Platt Cannon and over the range into the South Park, and to Fairplay, and then beyond to - no one knew where. But even by the summer of 1878 it had gotten but fifty-nine miles from Denver. Meanwhile the Denver and Rio Grande Railway, "The great scenic route" of today was running a little "jerk water" train from Denver to Pueblo, and a branch to Canon City. The opening up of Leadville, with its great possibilities in passenger freight and

....

1 Hall, Vol. III, P. 447

2 Con Cunningham - confirmed by others.

ore traffic produced a grand struggle between these lines to see who could reach the wonder first. There also occurred in the fall of 1878, a great battle between the Denver and Rio Grande and the Santa Fe, for the possession of the right of way through the Royal Gorge. Several men were killed in pitch battle; the case was then taken to court and after bitter struggle, the Rio Grand won out. The cost of the section of the road was enormous and was $100,000 a mile for a portion of the distance.[1]

The South Park meantime had reached Welster by the fall of 1878, the following April to Como; in August it reached Weston, and by February 1880 its lines ran into Buena Vista, but 37 miles from Leadville and this for a while was the railroad center of the Carbonate Camp. By July the Rio Grande had built up the Arkansas Valley and gave it a joint trackage to Leadville where it arrived in August. This gave the Cloud City two lines to Denver, one by way of the South Park, 184 miles long; the other around by Canon City and Pueblo, 278 miles in length. Both lines immediately did an immense business. A determined effort was made by the citizens of Malta to prevent by injunction, etc.. the railroad coming from that place to Leadville. These people had an idea that if Malta could be made the railroad center of the lead and silver country, that it would be a second Chicago, the railroad metropolis of the far west; however, their

....

[1] Fossett, P. 417

attempts came to complete failure.[1]

The advent of the railroad in Leadville was hailed with joy, and considered a guarantee of everlasting prosperity. The first distinguished person to arrive over the new line was General Grant, accompanied by his wife, Mrs. Fred Grant and child, and Governor Smith and wife of Wisconsin. This was on the evening of July 22, 1880. "The streets were a blaze of splendor". A magnificent banquet was held the evening of the 24th at the Clarendon. Grant spoke on his first impressions of Leadville. Some years later the Rio Grande was changed to standard gage, and connected with the transcontinental systems.[2]

In 1881 a street car line from Chestnut Street to the Rio Grande depot was established. The cars were drawn by horses but the line only remained in existence a relatively short time In 1888 the Midland Railway made its entrance into Leadville.

The banking history of Leadville is unique. The first bank was established in the spring of 1878 as the Lake County Bank, but because of increased business, it was recognized under the Federal Laws with a capital stock of $60,000 and the name changed to the First National Bank.[3] Its officers were: J.F. Eshelman, President; F.A.Reynolds, Vice-President; J.W.Zollars, Cashier. Its exchange business for 1879 amounted to $10,000,000. The bank of Leadville commenced business on the 15th of October 1878 with a capital stock of $50,000. Its officers were:

....

[1]Hall, Vol.II, Pages 466-and 470. Con Cunningham, James Knight in Elks Convention Pamphlet, Carbonate Weekly Chronicle, Jan. 1, 1881, P. 1 and 7; and C.C.Davis.

[2]Carbonate Weekly Chronicle, Jan. 1, 1881, P. 15

[3] Fossett, P. 417

Tabor, President; August Rische, Vice-President; George R. Fisher, Cashier. Its deposits for 1880 amounted to $61,000,000; its exchange $16,000,000, and at the end of the year had a surplus of $50,000. The Miners Exchange Bank, situated on Chestnut Street, was started April 17, 1878, and is perhaps older by several weeks than the Lake County Bank. It was organized by Messrs. James H.B.McFerrna, George Timble, and A.V.Hunter, with a capital stock of $25,000 to start with. The Merchants and Mechanics Bank started in 1879 by Messrs. L.M. and L.J. Smith, with a capital stock of $25,000. The City Bank, with a capital of $50,000 was organized June 24, 1880, by a stock company. J. W. Flaxan was President; C.C.Howell, Vice-President; John Kerr, Cashier; C.P.Shoemaker, Teller. In 1881 and 1882 all of these banks got to speculating heavily in mining stocks, etc., and in 1883 and 1884 everyone of them went broke. The City Bank was opened largely by Easterners and they liquidated and paid off their depositers. The Bank of Leadville, the largest in the city, went absolutely bankrupt July 27, 1883. In the following year the First National and Merchants and Mechanics failed,both substantially brankrupted. This resulted in the town being without a bank. Then the Carbonate Bank, a State Bank, founded by those who had been largely depositors in the Bank of Leadville, and in 1884 Hunter again started in banking. In 1887 the Carbonate was nationalized and in 1888 the Carbonate National and Hunter combined,with David H.Duggan, President, Hunter, Vice-President, Geo. Tumble, Cashier. Shortly prior to this, the American National was organized by B.H.Williams, Charles T.

Limberg, Sherman and others. For several years these were the only two banks in town; then Peter W. Breen organized the Leadville Savings and Deposit Bank, but this quit in 1898, leaving again only two in operation.[1]

Church history for Lake County started with Father Robinson. He built a church at Fairplay in 1872. He made frequent visits to California Gulch. The first Mass was held there in June 1873 in Tom Starr's blacksmith shop, with the anvil used as the altar. The congregation consisted of all denominations.[2] Father Robinson came often to the gulch, was present at many a christening, wedding, and smoothed the pillar for many a departed one. Years later when Leadville came into existence, he was the first parish priest here, and it was due to his energy and rustling powers that the big Catholic Church at the corner of Seventh and Popular Streets was erected. This, the Church of the Annunciation, was dedicated New Years Day 1880. Father Robinson also gave valuable aid to the Sisters of Charity and helped them raise the funds for St. Vincent's Hospital. In February 1878 the Reverend Thomas A. Uzzell came to camp; held meetings in a log cabin in the rear of the Grand Hotel, West Chestnut Street. He solicited funds, much of which was donated by saloon men and gamblers, and built the Methodist Church, which was the first Protestant Church in Leadville, at the corner of West Third and Spruce. W.H.Stevens donated four lots and $200 towards it;

....

[1]Fossett, P. 417 - Hist. Arkansas Valley, P.256-257. New Years Edition of Leadville Chronicle and Herald Democrat. Peter W. Breene. Leadville and the Gold Belt, P. 115. Carbonate Weekly Chronicle, Jan. 1, 1881, P. 17

[2]Con Cunningham and Mrs. Starr.

Tabor gave the chandeliers, and Captain Cooper gave the bell. This Church was completed July 5, 1878. St. George's Episcopal Church was organized during 1879, under the able direction of Rev. T.J.Mackay. Plans were made for the present magnificent church on the corner of West Fourth and Pine, which was completed in 1881 at the cost of $18,000. The Hebrew Benevolent Association was organized October 19, 1879, although their church was not completed until September 1894. The Presbyterian, Baptists, Congregationalists, all organized during 1878 and have since erected splendid and commodious houses of worship.[1]

In the very early history of the camp, schools were established, but of necessity had to be held in cabins and halls or any rooms that could be obtained. The first public school was opened in July 1877 with Miss Lottie Williams as teacher. She taught two months and received $200. In the fall of 1878 a board of directors was organized, and a school started in February 1878, which lasted for three months with an average attendance of 22 pupils. Louise H. Updegraff was teacher and the school was a log cabin located at 124 Elm Street. In May the citizens voted a school fund of $1700. A fair frame building was put up on the site now forming a portion of the grounds at Central School, at a cost of $3000. Two instructors were employed and about 60 pupils enrolled. The next year saw the start of the boom days. This necessitated the hiring of more teachers, and a high school was soon started, now known as the Central School.

....

[1] Leadville and the Gold Belt, P. 107-109.

It was completed May 14, 1881. Before the close of the year, 1219 pupils were enrolled. In July 1881 contracts were let for the Ninth Street School building, a duplicate of the Central School. Provisions were also made for schools at Carbonate Hill and Seventh Street. The Modern High School was completed in April 1900. In 1912 more room was needed and the Annex was purchased. For the school year, 1915-1916 there were 248 pupils enrolled in the High School, with a faculty of 9 teachers, exclusive of a music and drawing, a domestic science, and a manual training teacher, and a school total enrollment of 1330 with 46 teachers.[1]

The first newspaper "Reville", a Republican Weekly was started in an old log cabin in California Gulch in the spring of 1879. The editor and manager being R.S.Allen, known as "Dick" by everyone in camp. The plant was brought in from Fairplay, being packed over the range on burros. Three months later, Will Hogan brought in the camp a country plant from Alma and started a Democratic Weekly, called the "Eclipse". Dr. John Law had owned it at Alma but sold to Hogan who was responsible for bringing it here. A few months later he sold to Geo. T. Wanless, who rechristened it "The Eclipse News". In October 1878, it was announced in Denver that Messrs. Aikens, Burnell and Davis of the "Denver Tribune" were to start a daily paper at Leadville. This announcement caused the owners of the Eclipse and the Reville to start dailies at once. Unfortunately, both

....

[1] Leadville and the Gold Belt, P. 114-115. Supt. of Schools, George Hammers.

took the morning field, leaving the afternoon open for the Denver men. This new paper called the "Chronicle" put out its first issue January 29, 1879. They commenced printing at 3:00 P.M. and turned out 1500 papers an hour until 9 P.M., when the office was cleared of people begging for a copy. The same night an order was sent in for more material and before it reached Leadville a second order was sent. Frequently the daily sale ran as high as 7000 copies. The office was located on Harrison Avenue and was the first building north of State Street. This was outside of the city limits, but the proprietors finding it impossible to secure insurance, and not supposing the city would ever reach that far, thought they were avoiding all danger of fire by selecting this location. The office had a power press, but since there was no power, men were employed at $1.00 per hour to turn it by hand. But labor was scarce and frequently even the manager and editor had to "take a turn at the wheel". There was only one telegraph line at the time, running into Leadville, and this was so essential to the Chronical that we find that whenever the wire was down, the whole force including the editor would turn out to help repair it. Great difficulty was met with in securing supplies; frequently paper was on the road sixty days, but the Chronical never missed an issue though more than once the last sheet was on the feed board when the fresh supply arrived.[1]

....

1 Leadville and the Gold Belt, P. 119 -125. James Knight in Elk's Convention Pamphlet. C.C.Davis. History Arkansas Valley, P. 253-256.

The Chronicle cleared $50,000 the first year. The sale of the daily was tremendous, but greatly passed by the weekly. Davis writes "the standing order of four local news dealers called for 10,000 copies of that publication, while other venders took a smaller amount. The price to dealers was seven cents; to the public ten cents. Wagon loads went out each week to every quarter of the globe and not a few to Europe. It was regularly kept on file at the Paris office of the New York Herald, the Anglo-American Bank, and similar public places in the chief cities of the continent. The special editions, sent out on the first of each January, met with astonishing sales. The first venture in this line was on New Year's Day 1880. It was patterned after such publications as the Ladies' Home Journal, printed on fine calendered book paper, and profusely illustrated with half-tones of scenes typical of mining camps and mining camp life. The home facilities for such a publication were wholly inadequate; hence I contracted with the New York Graphic, the first illustrated daily in the country, for the printing. When all other details had been arranged, I was asked how many copies would be required, and when I said sixty thousand, the Graphic man gasped with astonishment. He declared that twenty-five thousand copies of the holiday number of the Graphic was all the metropolis of the country would consume. Sixty thousand for a wild and woolly mining camp, on the dome of the continent, was to him unthinkable; and I later learned that before signing the contract, he enquired of my bank references, not only as to my financial standing, but as to my sanity. However, I knew the

people and the market, and my judgement was confirmed on New Year's Day following, by the sale of the last number before the sun went down over Mount Massive. The retail pricewas fifty cents a copy; news dealers' rate was thirty-five cents. One dealer, Ben Gardner, later a prominent statesman of Los Angeles, handed us a check on New Year's Eve for $3,500 for ten thousand copies, and this before even seeing a sample copy. The Chronicle job office also did a tremendous business and showed a great profit."[1]

Eugene Field then editor of The Denver Tribune explained the way The Chronicle did business, as follows: A gambler desired some numbers 1 to 0 printed in big type on cardboard, for use in a game of chance of questionable sort. Characteristic of that liberal class, the gambler neglected to ask the price, and Burnell entered the order on his job register, fixing the charge at $10. Davis scanning the register, noted the entry and demurred to the price, declaring that they would be justified in holding up such a disreputable character as the one in question. Burnell changed the charge price from $10 to $20. Enter Arkens, who is appealed to by Burnell, for justification of the charge. "Sure" replies Arkens, "He is a disreputable whelp, deserving no consideration. Besides he'll pay $30 as quickly as $20." The charge price is again changed. Then Whitton, the circulator, comes in Burnell inquiries about the gambler. "Know him?" replies Whitton. "I should say I do.

....

[1] Davis, P.129-130

"Why, he's an escaped convict from the Dakota Penitentiary. If you're doing work for him, slap on the price. He is in an unlawful business, and will not dare to squeal". Advised as to the charge, and successive raises, Whitton finally advised making it $50. To this Burnell agreed, providing Whitton would deliver the goods and make the collection. After satisfying himself that the cards have been correctly printed, the gambler draws a check for $50 and hands it to Whitton without a word, but as the latter turns to depart, he is hailed by the Bad Man from Dakota with "John, I was a thief once myself you know, but isn't this price a little high?"[1]

Davis writes that he believes The Chronicle was the first newspaper in America to employ a female reporter. Kate Williams was her name.[2] Also that he paid more for having print paper hauled from Denver to Leadville than the rate would have been from Liverpool to Portland around the horn.[3]

Seth Paine was one of the editors in 1879. He was a very striking and original character and a very proficient writer. He had served time in New Jersey for writing criminal libel. A sample of his work on The Chronical is as follows: Andrew Johnson, an escaped convict of the Kansas Penitentiary, arrived in town last night and is stopping at No. 10233 Chestnut Street. Then would follow a description of Andrew. Another time he wrote an article describing the pompous appearance and majestic

....

1 Davis, P. 133-134

2 Davis, P. 178

3 Davis, P. 320.

entrance of a minister into the dining room of the Clarendon Hotel, and a list of things ordered by him, showing he had a great capacity for food. The minister was so thoroughly humiliated that he left the camp.[1]

The Chronical conducted a spirited fight against all thieves and other crooks. Large bribes were offered if they would quit, and threats made to burn the office if they did not. This resulted in fortifying the office and preparations were made for battle. However, no fight occurred. By this time both the "Reville" and the "Eclipse" were on their last legs and soon ceased publishing. In October 1879 a group of wealthy and influential local citizens formed the "Herald Printing Company" with a capital stock of $20,000. Its incorporators included W.H.James (first mayor of Leadville), Edward Eddy Bush, and C.I.Thompson, a prominent lawyer. The first editor was R. J. Dill. Both the "Chronical" and the "Herald" achieved success from the start. In 1880 Davis bought out Burnell's and Arken's interest in the Chronical and they returned to Denver. When Tabor became a candidate for the U.S.Senate he bought the Herald Republican from the Old Herald Printing Company, and it is said that it cost Tabor $65,000 a year to run it. Meanwhile the Democratic Party, finding itself in need of an organ, formed the Democratic Printing Company and put out its first issue January 1, 1880. The company was capitalized at $25,000. W.H.Robinson was business manager, but W.A.H.Loveland, afterwards part owner of the Denver News, was the leading spirit. In

....

[1] James Knight.

1881 The Time Printing Company, with a capital stock of $15,000 was established but only lasted a few months. Other papers that only sprang up to die out soon were "The Chestnut Street Boom", "The Leadville Circular", "The Leadville News", a labor paper published by Geo. Clarke during the strike of 1880, "The Leadville Journal", "The Dispatch", and many others. In 1883 C.C. Davis bought the "Democrat" and consolidated it with the "Chronicle". In 1886 James McCarthy purchased the Herald Republican from Tabor and a few days later sold it to Davis, who now united them under the name of the "Herald Democrat". Said paper has been issued under that name ever since and thus completes the unique newspaper history of the city.[1]

The first post office was in Tabor's store at Oro. Mrs. Tabor was postmistress, and the facilities consisted of rather irregular connections with Denver. The carriers went down one week and tried to come back the next. Postage was fifty cents a letter. Next we find the post office consisted of a cigar box in Charles Mater's store. Then early in 1878 we find Meyer, Harrison, Tabor, and others petitioning for a post office, which was established early that year. Henderson was selected postmaster, and the office was located in the 200 Block on West Chestnut. Later the office was moved near to where Elk's Opera House stands today; then to 501 Harrison; then 608 Harrison; then the Government building was built and the

....

[1] James Knight

office moved to its present site. During the busy days of 1879 A.A. Smith was postmaster. The office then was a wonder and did a larger local business than any office between Kansas City and San Francisco. Early in the year '79, the daily business was $1,000 for sale of stamps; 8,000 letters received; 6,000 forwarded; and the average value of money orders was $20,000 a week. Business increased about 40% a month. Postmaster Smith had thirteen clerks and the whole force was overworked. Business increased so rapidly that he was forced to secure more help and at his own expense. There were four delivery windows and there was often, particularly on Sunday, four long lines extending for over a block. Sometimes as many as 600 waiting, often from $1 to $5 was paid to obtain a place in the line, only to have the window slammed in their face when their turn had almost arrived. Boys and even men made "wages" by securing a position in the waiting line. Mud was often six inches deep, after a rain, in front of the post office, but in an hour it was hard from the crowds walking on it. In 1880 the total receipts amounted to $811,876.75.[1]

The telgraph office also did a tremendous business. From a financial point of view the Western Union Telegraph office in Leadville was the most important in the State. The receipts totaled $41,485.89; the messages sent number 70,614 and those received 65,447.[2]

....

1 Fossett, P. 417; - Con Cunningham, P.G.Goris, C.H.S.Whipple, Judge Cavender and Judge McLaird.

2 Fossett, P. 417; - History Arkansas Valley, P. 256.

The Smelting history of Leadville is remarkable. No mining camp in the world was ever, in so short a period provided with as many extensive melting works. The old Malta works were the first ever erected in Lake County. They were built in the spring of 1875 by Professor E. Loeschn and others, to treat ores from the Homestake Mine, Carbonates being then unknown in the camp. After 1877, the works were closed, then let to numerous leasers, operated but a small portion of the time, and finally closed. The Harrison Reduction Works put in operation in October 1877 was the first smelter in Leadville proper. This was followed by twelve others. The Grant Smelter was the largest, and their output in 1880 nearly equaled any other two. This was started September 23, 1878. The La Plata had been erected the previous June, but the furnace had not been started until October. In 1879 the Billing and Eilers, the California, J.B.Dickson, Ohio and Missouri, Cummings and Finn, Eddy James and Company, Elgin, etc., were started. The total production of shipments for 1878 had amounted to a little over $3,000,000. In 1879 they totaled $10,500,000, while in 1880 they had risen to over $15,000,000. In that year the individual output was as follows:

The Grant Smelting Company ---- ----------------	4,018,290
Eddy, James & Company -------------------------	1,363,334
La Plata ---------------------------------------	2, 316,510
Leadville --------------------------------------	14,218
American ---------------------------------------	299,126
Billings & Eilers ------------------------------	2,105,701
California -------------------------------------	702,826
J.B.Dickenson & Co. ----------------------------	63,961
Little Chief -----------------------------------	109,072
Taylor & Buentan Mill --------------------------	62,200
Ohio & Missouri --------------------------------	822,656

Cummings & Finn	1,324,213
Gage, Hagaman & Co.	213,697
Oro Stamp Mill	3,438
Malta Works	24,362
Tabor Mill	11,250
Elgin Mining & Smelting Co.	462,439
Harrison Reduction Works	917,304
Robert E. Lee	114,318
Colorado Prince Mill	22,000
Gulch Mines	70,000
	$ 15,040,715[1]

Although there were 14 smelters in 1880, by the 90's there were but two; however, their total output was equal to the fourteen and their processes and handling was far cheaper. At the present time there is but the Arkansas Valley; however, its business is tremendous and efficiently handled.[2]

In 1877 before the city was named, Thomas Harris was appointed first marshall, with two assistants. He held office until April 1878 when the first city council elected George O'Connor, who was killed a month later in Bill Nye's gambling house by James Bloodswalk. Mart Duggan was then chosen and finished out the unexpired time; i.e, until April 1879, when P.A.Kelly was appointed. He served until November, then resigned and Mart again was elected. In April 1880 E.H.Watson was elected. He raised the force to 36 men and worked them in the eight hour shift, each shift in charge of a competent man. This force made up of carefully picked and extremely competent men. All were thoroughly drilled, in their duties, military tactics, and cavalry; all kept themselves in splendid physical

....

1 New Year Edition - Leadville Chronicle, Jan. 1, 1881
2 Judge Cavender, James Knight.

shape, and all were handy with the 45 caliber revolver which each carried. As the conditions have become more quiet, the number has been greatly reduced.[1]

Early in 1878 a bucket brigade was organized to fight fires; then a salt water wagon was stationed on the corner of Harrison and Chestnut to be used to dip water from in case of fire. In June of that year the necessity of greater equipment led to the forming of the Harrison Hook and Ladder Company, Number 1, with the motto "We strive to save". Its officers consisted of Edwin Harrison, James S. Pridy, Maxey Tabor, Frank Gay, H.A.W. Tabor, etc. This company did splendid service. Its first fires were the Coliseum Theatre on Chestnut, the block opposite the Clarendon, and the great fire at the corner of Chestnut and the Avenue. In March 1879 was formed the Tabor Hose Company No. 1. Tabor presented them with their first hose carriage. Soon after the Bush Hose Company organized, but disbanded in 1880; later succeeded by the Humphry Hose Company. In 1882 a paid department was organized with 18 fully paid firemen. The department has done splendid work, and there has only been one serious accident, that in 1883 when Messrs. Malloy and McCune were crushed at the Grand Central fire. In the summer of 1887 there was held in Leadville a big firemens' tournament; teams were here not only from all over the state, but from many cities far outside the state. The time for a few days resembled the Rush Days of '79;

....

1 See previous chapter.

several men were shot, drunken fights common, and a wild holiday in general. However, the Tabor Hose Company, with Wm. J. Allen at its head, landed the World's Championship by performing the dry test, 600 feet in $30\frac{1}{5}$ seconds; the wet test, 700 feet in $32\frac{4}{5}$ seconds; and the straight away in 26 seconds.[1]

In December 1879 a company of militia under the name of the Tabor Mine Guards was organized. It consisted of about 35 young men. During the strike of 1880, it did splendid service; although continually on duty, always at the place of danger, yet thanks to the discretion of its officers, no blood was shed. After the strike they were mustered out of service and immediately the organization of the Tabor Light Cavalry was completed. The company was mustered into state service for three years. Its officers were Captain, J.D.McCarthy; First Lieutenant, George D. Lyles; Second Lieutenant, Peter R. Hull.[2]

In 1882 Leadville had a base ball team with a national reputation. The Leadville Blues, as they were called, led by John D. Morgan and Harry Kellogg, who travelled throughout the country and played in many of the big Eastern cities against Major League Teams and made a remarkable record. Later a number of the players won a place on big Eastern Nines.[3]

A Leadville band was organized in 1879 and has been in existence ever since, with varying successes, but on the whole a rather creditable record.[4]

....

[1]Leadville & The Gold Belt, P. 105, supplemented by members of the department.

[2]New Year Edition - Leadville Chronicle, Jan. 1, 1881

[3] and [4]Leadville newspapers

On the eighteenth of March 1879, the Leadville Gas Company filed its charter. A large amount of money was put into the plant, and soon a high grade of gas was being furnished the city and citizens for street and home lighting. The Water Works System was also established in 1879. Electric lighting was established soon afterwards, and telephones were in use almost from the start.[1]

Before closing this Chapter, I want to recall the fact that it was Leadville that made Denver, and practically Colorado. When Carbonates were discovered in Leadville, Denver was quite a dying city of not more than 15,000 people; it had but a single car line, no great buildings, and no prospects. Its merchants spent much of the time in poker playing in the streets; the jack rabbit could be hunted within the city limits; the favored topic of conversation was "The Days of '59", which were gone forever; but with the Rush to Leadville in '79, Denver enjoyed a boom that far out-rivaled the days of the gold rush. Crowds poured in to the city. The merchants forgot to talk of '59; they were too busy sending goods to Leadville. Many a man who made a fortune in the Carbonate Camp returned to Denver to build. Tabor early erected the Tabor Grand Opera House, the first theatre at that time west of Chicago. He alone drew thousands to Denver, many of whom stayed. And with regards to her millionaires, many owe their fortunes to the Cloud City and while Denver may "knock" Leadville as only a mining camp, yet it fully realizes what it owes to the Carbonate Rush and Production of 1879.[2]

....

1 History Arkansas Valley, P. 257

2 James Knight - confirmed by C.H.S.Whipple, et el.

For example, Lincoln H. Hall wrote in his History of Cripple Creek in 1896. "The outpouring of the precious metal from Leadville transformed the struggling Centennial State into a veritable autocrat in the Colony of States. As if by magic the rough frontier town of Denver became a metropolis; stately buildings arose on the site of shanties; crystal streams flowed through the arid plains and the desert blossomed and became fruitful. Poverty gave way to the annoyance of wealth and the fame of the Silver State spread throughout the World".[1]

....

[1]L.H.Hall, "Cripple Creek District Up-to-Date", P.4

CHAPTER VI

THE SUBSTANTIAL MINING PERIOD

The excitement, the glories, the stampede of the Rush Days. were brought to an end by a series of unexpected, though not illogical, events in the spring of 1880. As stated previously, the Little Pittsburgh had been incorporated in 1879 for $20,000,000, and so eager were the Eastern investors for western mining stock that one-fourth of the stock was soon disposed of in New York for a million dollars, but the ideasin regard to the extent of ore and value of the property were extravagant. The sales of stock upon the New York Exchange were enormous and rapid. Of all the stock dealt in, that of the Little Pittsburgh was the most desired, and soon rose to $35 and $40 a share. Tabor had parted with his stock in September. Moffat and Chaffer were now the chief holders. They based their opinions upon personal investigations, and the opinion of the best mining experts was that the property was without limit. However, the heavy demand of dividends of $100,000 a month were depleting the ore deposits faster than they could be opened up.[1]

Then in February 1880 came the appalling news from Superintendent H.B.Bearce that the paying bodies were worked out and that dividends must be suspended while new bodies were located. Finding that the report was true and the secret could not be kept, Moffat flooded the market with stock. Soon the exposure and crash came. Stock fell from $35 to $6. This greatly affected all other mining companies and there was a sudden decline in

....

[1]Carbonate Weekly Chronicle, Jan. 1, 1881, P. 1.

Leadville stocks, the advances of capital were stopped and the spirit of enterprise was checked. This practically killed the camp, and there was a feeling that the whole excitement had been superficial after all.[1] Then in the last of May occurred the great labor strike. The miners struck for four dollars a day and an eight hour shift. (They had been receiving $3 for dry work and $3.50 for working where it was wet). The strike was lead from the first to the last by a bold, energetic, intelligent Irishman named Mooney, and it was he who made the strike one of gigantic dimensions. Frank Hall, in his excellent history of Colorado, writes "Negotiations between the malcontents and managers followed, but both being obstinate, nothing came of them; as a consequence the strike spread to all the principal mines, the workmen walked out and crowded into the town, organized a procession with a brass band at the head and marched to the various shafts, where such as were at work were called out and joined them. While no acts of violence occurred, the demonstrations were powerful and alarming. The less prudent uttered threats against life and prosperity". Mooney held his miners well in hand. The excitement was intense. The stoppage of work, the marching procession, the fighters, all added to the excitement and fear of danger. The business men and citizens organized and decided upon a tremendous parade. This was staged but nearly resulted in bloodshed. The miners instead of being overawed, were indignant and irritated to the fighting point. Serious

....

[1] Hall, Vol. 2, P. 456-457.

trouble was only prevented by the police and a company of militia, who cleared the streets. This affair caused the better citizens to appeal to Governor Atkin for military aid. The Governor was extremely reluctant to interfer, but it seemed the only solution. Hence, he sent in state troops, under the command of William H. James, and issued an order declaring martial law. The effect was magical. At once the town became quiet. General James issued his orders and all obeyed him. All classes respected him and aided him in restoring order. The strike ended on June 18, and a week later, June 26, the men resumed work; therefore, just one month after the miners walked out, the strike was over. Reliable gossip has it that the strike was caused by certain mine owners, who desired a reason for the non-payment of dividends. For example, the Chrysolite had struck a vein estimated at tremendous values; this had caused their stock to rise 600 to 800%, and later it was found that the vein was only a few feet wide.[1]

However, the collapse of the Little Pittsburgh, carrying with it other companies, and the strike, ended the boom period of Leadville. The result was desirable. It swept away the unhealthy, the gamblers, the toughs, and the non-producers. It resulted in substantial mining, under careful management, the most approved and economic methods. It established legitimate procedure in every channel of business and industry. The mine owners either developed or leased their holdings to

....

[1]Hall, Vol. 2, P. 460-464; History Arkansas Valley, P.239-245. Carbonate Weekly Chronicle, Jan. 1, 1881. Judge Cavender. James McNeece

experienced miners. The camp settled down to a quiet, substantial production of ore. New sources and new metals were discovered and the long years of production that have given Leadville its reputation were inaugurated.[1]

The year 1879 had witnessed a production of $10,333,740.69 with silver and lead the leaders; the following year in spite of the playing out of the rich mines on Fryer Hill and the strike, the total production reached $15,095,153.00. The next year witnessed a great shrinkage in the population of the camp and mining activity, but still the production was kept at $13,170,576.00. The year 1882 was the banner year, with a production of $17,131,853.00, followed the next year with nearly as much, $15,839,446.00. By this time the population and activity of the camp had fallen still lower. Thousands of people had left the camp. Population was probably about 15,000. There were many indications, as many believed, that the end of the marvelous riches had come.[2]

It began to be painfully evident that every hole sunk in the ground for a couple of hundred feet was not developing a bonanza and the superficial miner began to grow discouraged. There were, of course, a good many paying mines. The Iron-Silver, the Maid and Henriette, the Fryer Hill bonanzas, and some of the others were keeping up the magnificent reputation of the camp. Still the edge of the boom had worn off; the effervescence was disappearing, and the mining business was rapidly settling

....

1 Judge Cavender - James Knight.

2 New Year Editions - Leadville Herald and Leadville Chronicle.

down to its normal condition. It was, of course, realized by the prominent mining men in the 80's that if the mining deposits were confined to the outcrop veins, the future of the camp was by no means assured. This fact alone had a dampening effect on even the most enthusiastic; although the far-sighted mining men were not ready to concede that with the exhaustion of the rich surface deposits the mining possibilities of the district were ended.[1]

In 1884 the production had fallen to $12,837,497.00. It was a half million less or $12,357,662, the next year, with a slight rise to $13,750,733.30 in 1886; back to $12,072,967.81 in 1887, and down to $11,605,205.48 in 1888. The year 1889 witnessed a slight rise to $13,639,351.75, but 1890 produced but $11,798,892.84.[2]

During the later 80's, many of the large companies, particularly the famous old ones, located on Fryer Hill, had stopped active operations, and had turned their property over to lessees. These lessees covered every hill in the camp, and a great many of them were making good money, principally in carbonates and iron. And it was due to the activity of the lessees that the old mines were kept open and that the upper contacts on Carbonate Iron, Fryer and Rock Hills were exposed.[3]

....

[1]Elks Convention Pamphlet, 1907, under "The First Set-back".
[2]New Year Editions of Herald - Democrat. Also Leadville and the Gold Belt, P. 91
[3] Elks Convention Pamphlet; under "The First Set-back".

There was also a great movement towards formation of larger mining companies with greater problems. The encountering of water was one of these problems. The Maid and Henrietta were the first that met with this great subterraneous water basin as its shaft was sunk into the lower contact. Heavy pumps were used to remove this obstacle, but it was clearly proven that the ore values below the water level justified the tremendous expenditure. And soon other mines began their deep shafts. Among these were the Mahala, Small Hopes, etc.[1] About this same time, Campion and others conceived the idea that the ore did not end at the edge of the hills, and they sunk what is known as the Elk Shaft west of the Carbonate fault, and discovered large bodies of ore there, which to a degree resurrected the camp. Other discoveries followed, among them the Penrose, Great Eagle, Coronado, and others now know as the down-town mines.[2]

The big producers throughout this period were the Henrietta and Maid who in 1890 totaled 55,000 tons; the A.Y. and Minnie, with a total of 40,000 tons; the Col. Sellers with 39,827 tons; the Flagstaff with 21,000 tons; the Iron-Silver, including Mayer, 18,000 tons; and the Morning and Evening Star with 18,000; the Matchless 18,000; The Breece, 18,720; the Continental Chief 12,480; Dunkin, 15,174, and Elk, 12,730.[3]

There were at that time few smelters in active operation; American Smelting Company who in 1890 handled 65,000 tons valued

....

1 Elks Convention Pamphlet; under "The First Set-Back".
2 Judge Cavender.
3 New Years Edition - Leadville Herald Democrat, Jan.1, 1891

at $2,401,458.90; The Arkansas Valley Smelting Company who handled 66,429 tons valued at $2,382,743.17. The St. Louis Smelting and Refining Company, with 36,720 tons valued at $869,291.72; and the Elgin Smelting Company with 15,076 tons valued at $413,306.65. These smelters during this year handled over 34,000,000 pounds of lead and better than four and one-quarter million ounces of silver, with nearly 10,000 ounces of gold. Silver during 1890 ranged from 90 cents per ounce in value to 119.875 cents, while lead ran from $3.80 per 100 pounds to $5.25. This shows the relative value of the camp production in this period.[1]

The prosperous period of the camp lasted until the silver troubles in 1892. In 1891 the production was a shade better than that of 1890, or a total of 11,916,740, with silver selling from about 94 to 104; but before the end of the next year the set backs that ended this substantial quiet period of mining had set in.[2] However, the importance of this substantial period dating from the fall of 1880 to that of 1892, cannot be over-estimated. It lacked the excitement, the glories of the Rush Days, but it did much to strengthen Leadville's claim that it is the greatest mining camp in the world. Throughout the period Leadville attracted capital and attention throughout the world. It did much to build up the whole state as well as contribute to the nation. Millions taken from the Leadville mines were

....

1 and 2 New Year Editions - Leadville Herald Democrat.

used to erect business blocks in Denver and Chicago, the Grand Hotel at San Diego, the Flat Iron Building in New York, and to develop coal fields in West Virginia, oil land in Pennsylvania, etc.[1]

The Leadville region also played an important part in state politics. Although the city only had between four and five thousand votes, still it sent big delegations to all the conventions.[2]

However, the local government at Leadville was very corrupt. The fee system was in vogue, and Davis writes it resulted in the sheriff receiving $50,000 per annum; county clerk, $60,000; assessor, $30,000, etc. This caused unscrupulous men to spend fortunes in corrupting elections and resulted in poor officials, bad management, terrific corruption and graft.[3]

Until November 1892, Colorado had but one Congressional district, and the men that represented the state in the lower house at Washington from October 1877 to November 1892 were James B. Belford, Thomas M. Patterson, George C. Symes, and Hosea Townsend.[4]

Although Leadville long enjoyed the reputation of being the most wicked city in the world and boasted of some features in this connection[5]; it also held in high respect a good woman;

....

1 Judge Cavender, Peter W. Breene, James Knight, C.C.Davis, P. 311-312.
2 Hall, Vol. 2, P. 471.
3 Davis, P. 236-237
4 J.E.Snook, Col. History & Govt., P. 29.
5 See Carbonate Weekly Chronicle, Jan. 1, 1891, P. 4.

always contributed liberally to suffering humanity, religious works, and similar philanthropic objects. It is true, however, the first appeal was always made to the habitues of State Street, ninety-five percent of whom were gamblers, thieves, thugs, dance hall keepers, prostitutes, etc. No appeal to that element ever went unanswered or needed any urging.[1]

One event of great interest in this period was the visit of Chief Magistrate of the United States, President Harrison, and his suite, to the local mining camp, on Monday, May 11,1891. The city had been decorated beautifully for the occasion; the Star Spangled Banner flowed from hundreds of business buildings, residents, and shaft houses surrounding the mines that covered the hills. The scene was one which to use the words of the president himself was "calculated to inspire the dullest heart". Judge P.M.Goddard made the speech of welcome; the President responded and declared the scene from where he stood was "the highest evidence of American pluck to be found in the United States". The President was presented with a brick weighing seven pounds, made of Leadville silver .999 fine, and measuring 4 x 2½ x 1; an exact fac-simile of the silver bricks as they come from the refinery. Each member of his party was also presented with a Leadville souvenir spoon, a box of mineral specimens, native silver, etc.[2]

....

[1]Jan. 1, 1916. Colorado went dry; by that time State Street had been properly cleaned up.

[2]Leadville Herald Democrat - May 11, 1891; Davis, P. 242

The most impbrtant mining men throughout this period included: Tingley S. Wood, who was engaged in banking and financial business in Ohio and Illdnois when the first notes of the great carbonate excitement at Leadville swept over the country. He immediately joined the travellers for the new Eldorado. Upon arriving in Leadville, he took hold of the Little Chief in 1880. Later he managed the Silver Cord, the Big Pittsburgh, was President of the Agwall Mining Company and interested in other holdings. He was always a strong advocator of scientific mining methods.[1]

James A. Shinn, another representative of a successful mining man, came here in 1879. He was superintendent of the Silver Cord for seven years and manager of the White Cap. for six years. Later he was Vice-President of the White Cap and Selma Companies; President of the Cleveland Gold Mining Company, and Vice-President of the Kisawlee Mining Company.[2]

Eben Smith first engaged in mining in California in 1852; in May 1860 he came to Gilpin County, Colorado and engaged in mining there. He was later interested in banking business in Denver; then in 1883 came to Leadville and took charge of the Louisville, but made his greatest reputation as manager of the great Maid of Erin Consolidation, when that property was at its fullest glory.[3]

....

[1]Leadville and the Gold Belt, P. 96
[2]Leadville and the Gold Belt, P. 99
3 Leadville and the Gold Belt, P. 98.

James J. Brown raised as a coal miner in Pennsylvania, but in the late 70's came to the Black Hills, then to the Deadwood diggings. In April 1880 he came to Leadville. He prospected at Aspin, Alma, Fairplay, and Red Cliff; then returned to Leadville and acted as Superintendent for Moffat and Smith for ten years. He was one of the largest owners in the Ibex Mining Company and spent years persistently exploring that property. He was also interested in mining property in Arizona, Montana, and Utah.[1]

James T. Briggs, one of the pioneers in the famous Venango Oil regions in Pennsylvania, visited Colorado in 1875. He bought the Black Prince Mine on Breece Hill in 1879. Retiring from the oil business, he settled in Leadville and devoted his interest to the developing of the Black Prince.[2]

Terry Conners came to Colorado in 1875, and to Leadville in September 1877. He opened the first two hundred feet of the south incline on the Iron-Silver Mine. In the spring of 1878 he became superintendent of the famous Gallapher Mine. Later he became interested in White Cap and other properties.[3]

John K. and S. Marshall Carleton were two early prospectors. They had studied minerology and mining engineering in New England; then in the fall of 1877 they came to Leadville and

....

[1]Leadville and the Gold Belt, P. 96
[2]Leadville and the Gold Belt, P. 99.
[3]Leadville and the Gold Belt, P.100.

opened an assay office on Chestnut Street. They also became interested in prospecting and located the Carleton Lode, the Portland and Walcott, the Marshall group on Long and Derry Hill, and the Capitol, Clipper, Castle and Congress lodes within the city limits.[1]

Major A. V. Bohn, born in Ohio, worked in the Lead Mines of Illinois, ran a store in Wisconsin, served throughout the Civil War, then interested in coal business in the West, and finally in February 1878 came to Leadville. He was manager of the Small Hopes, Matchless, Lucy B. Hussey, Shields, Star of Hope properties. Also was extensively interested in holdings of his own.[2]

Gusham F. North came to Leadville in 1878, engaged in leasing, then Superintendent of the Wolftone for three years. Later he turned to leasing and became interested in various properties.[3]

Charles North came to Leadville in 1881, managed property for Charles Hill and earned a reputation as a successful operator . Later he was manager of the Crescent Mine, and connected with other holdings.[4]

Robert O'Neil came to Leadville in 1879. He was master mechanic for the Maid of Erin, Small Hopes, and other properties. Later he was interested in the Rix and other properties.[5]

....

[1]Leadville and the Gold Belt, P. 98
[2]Leadville and the Gold Belt, P. 99
[3]Leadville and the Gold Belt, P. 100
[4] and [5]Leadville and the Gold Belt, P. 100.

John F. Campion came here in the carbonate period, managed the Elk, later the Little Johnny. He was one of the foremost mining authorities and held extensive interests.[1]

George W. Campion was a great hustler and interested during this period in more properties than any other man in camp, and most of them were successful. The discovery of ore in the Little Johnny shaft was indirectly due to him.[2]

Henry W. Smith did not come until 1887. Then, however, he demonstrated his ability as manager of the Henrietta and Louisville properties, and later became manager of the Grey Eagle and Pocahontas.[3]

A write-up of the leading mine operators of this period is far from complete without the mention of the name of a woman, Mrs. Augusta Tabor. We have already told of her early history, her coming with her husband to the Gulch, the long struggle during the sixties and seventies, and how Tabor became rich and a political power. Then when their star was at its height, the wife, who had labored by his side through the long years of hardship, was deserted by the mining king, and received but $300,000 out of Tabor's practically $10,000,000. However, Mrs. Tabor, by investments in mining property and careful management, increased her property tenfold; i.e, to $3,000,000 and died well-to-do, while her husband died virtually in poverty. Mrs. Tabor was loved and respected by all of the miners, and many, many of

....

1, 2, and 3 Leadville and the Gold Belt, P. 100

them remember her kindness and liberty with gratitude.[1]

....

[1]Leadville and the Gold Belt, P. 101-102.
Mines and Mining Men of Colorado, 1893, Published by John G.Canfield, Denver, gives a fuller account of the mines and men of this period.

CHAPTER VII

LEADVILLE BECOMES A GOLD CAMP

The substantial mining period, and the production of silver would perhaps have lasted indefinitely but for the sudden collapse of the silver market in 1893.

During the Rush Days, silver averaged about $1.15 per ounce. This during the 80's dropped somewhat, the average price being around 90 cents, but in 1890 when the Bland Allison Act, passed in 1878 and which provided for the purchase of silver bullion at the market price to the amount of from two to four million dollars worth each month for the purpose of coinage, was repealed, and the Sherman Act with its provision that the Secretary of the Treasury should purchase 4,500,000 ounces of silver each month, the price rose to 119.875 cents. This was the highest figure for silver in the history of the camp.

These monthly purchases, however, were to be paid for in silver certificates, but in order to keep them from depreciating, the Treasury Department had to redeem them in gold. This tended to exhaust the gold reserve rapidly and as government revenues were also falling off, owing to business depression, it could not be repleted. This exhaustion of the gold reserve indicated the early repeal of the "purchasing of silver", part of the Sherman Act, and with the approach of the business depression, the price of the white metal declined rapidly. In

1891 the price ranged from 90 to 104, in 1892 the average was 87½, in 1893 it had fallen to 78 cents.[1]

Then suddenly almost without a warning, on the 28th of June 1893, came the news that the British Government had closed the India mints to the coinage of silver. In August of the same year, Congress repealed the silver purchasing portion of the Sherman Act. Many a mining millionaire and merchant found himself ruined and the Leadville Camp was dead; deepest gloom settled on all. The feeling of the times was expressed in the following lines written by A. A. Blow and sung at the Consolation Dinner held at the Elks Club on July 1.[2]

Up in these mountains high and blue
   Listen to my tale of woe.
Dwells a shining metal of silver hue
   Which was freely coined in '72,
Into dollars on which the eagle flew
   Listen to my tale of woe.

Some prospectors one day tramping through
   Listened to my tale of woe
Sat down on the rocks their grub to chew.
   And there on the ground 'midst the grass and dew
Saw out crops of silver, which they knew,
   Listen to my tale of wee.

<u>Chorus:</u>

Hard trials - times look blue
   A silver dollar is not worth a sue
All on account of that Gold-Bug crew
   Oh, Listen to my tale of woe.

....

1 The daily price of silver can be secured from any daily paper issued in the mining states.

2 Davis, P. 446.

Then thousands of miners to these mountains flew,
Listen to my tale of woe
And thousands of miners began to hue
Out of these rocks where the silver grew
And wealth to all began to accrue
Listen to my tale of woe.

They founded railraods and cities too
Listen to my tale of woe
And millions of dollars into smelters blew
And built an empire vast and new
Which the Gold Bugs of earth can never subdue
But listen to my tale of woe.

Under free coinage now we'll set a jack screw
Listen to my tale of woe.
Turned by our backbone, brain, and sinew
And will fight like a desperate starved Zulu
To beat Grover Cleveland, the big Yahoo
Listen to my tale of woe.

Then we'll build a high wall 'long the big Mazoo
Listen to my tale of woe
And we'll fill to sinking a big canoe
With the monometallic Gold Bug Crew.
And sink them forever out of view
Listen to my tale of woe.

<u>Chorus:</u>

Hard trials, for the story is true
But better times will soon ensue
And we'll drink to the death of the Gold Bug Crew
Listen to my tale of woe.[1]

The oratorical and written attacks against the demonetization of silver and the repeal of the Sherman Act were extremely bitter. One editorial declared it a "treacherous blow struck the nation by a traitorous subject, effectually checking the prosperity of a region prolific of mineral, sufficient to feed the mammoth maw of industry for centuries. The appalling spectacle of the prostration of a district directly responsible for

....
[1]Davis, P. 446-448.

the elimination of the western frontier was presented -- a district whose resources lured the the evangel of progress into the rocky solitude of the great west and presented to civilization a christian commonwealth which reflects credit and glory upon the flag it embellishes. Sullied by savagery and ensconced in benightment, it was subjugated and reserved for a foul, cowardly fate. And in its darkest hour of trial, beset by the hellish minions of power, unable to ward off the barbed darts of anathema and vituperation; when its loyal sons made futile efforts to secure the cooperation of eastern friends who had absorbed the wealth of the district, their refusal furnished an apt illustration of man's inhumanity to man. They were sadly impervious to the sentiments of humanity and deaf to the appeals of distress."

However, Leadville at this time came forward with one more proof that it is the world's greatest mining camp. When the price of both silver and lead fell so suddenly in July 1893 the most sanguine could not help but admit the blow was ruinous if not absolutely fatal to the existence of the camp; for the price of silver was then supposed to be her only hope and salvation. The people, from owner to laborer, were downhearted. All were ready to quit. When suddenly, like a sky rocket through a clouded sky, came the Little Johnny on Breeze Hill, opening up large bodies of almost everything, gold, silver, lead, copper, and zinc.[1]

....

[1]A.A.Blow in Leadville and the Gold Belt, P. 71

The gold discovery immediately caused a new interest and led to great development. Tremendous activity began on Breeze Hill, the center of the gold belt. This was really not a new district. It was part of great silver and lead deposit that had been worked since 1879 and adjoins on the east the principal mines of the Leadville District, and had been worked on a small scale since 1879. However, the discovery immediately ushered in the Gold Era. The great Carbonate Camp because of unfavorable legislation now turned from its old love of silver and lead to gold.[1]

In 1893 the gold output of the district was but $803,200; the following year it totaled $1,934,240, and by 1895 there were dozens of gold producing mines in active operation, and new ones being constantly located. The daily output averaged 800 ounces, and the camp was the greatest gold producer in the state.[2]

In March alone one hundred and fourteen new mining companies were formed with a total capital of $350,000,000. Hundreds of claims were located, and in July there were sixty shafts and drill holes being sunk. These shafts and drill holes if added together would total over four miles. Four miles of holes, and as one writer has declared, every one determined to continue until gold, hot lemonade, or China, was struck. The camp surely was enjoying its third boom, even though it did not compare with that of 1860 or 1879.[3]

....

[1] Leadville and the Gold Belt, P. 73, 75, 78.
[2] Leadville and the Gold Belt, P. 79
[3] Leadville and the Gold Belt, P. 79

However, this boom was far different than the mad rush and scramble of 1879. This new kind of mining could not be carried on without capital. Leadville was no longer "a poor man's camp". Neither could there be a mad scramble for locations, conflicts, or armed disputes over prior rights, nor rich rewards gathered by lawyers from legal contentions. And all for the reason that the entire area is covered by United States patents, this shutting out litigation.[1]

Leadville in 1895 had an estimated population of 15,000.[2]

The principal mines were the Ibex, including the Little Johnny, which is probably the richest gold mine in the world today; the Golden Eagle, which adjoins the Ibex property; the Rex which struck gold in the spring of 1895 at a depth of 350 feet by means of a diamond drill. The Rex is located beyond the field of early developments, and for years it received little attention. The mines finally enlisted J. J. Brown, an experienced Leadville miner. Under his direction a diamond drill was placed at the bottom of a 200-foot shaft and boring started in the porphyry formation. The drill passed through one hundred feet of porphyry, six feet of talc, thirteen feet of intensive porphyry and nine feet of contact matter, when the core brought up gold ore and penetrated a body thirty-five feet thick, assays of which yielded as high as nine ounces of gold.[3]

....

[1]Leadville Herald Democrat, Jan. 1, 1894.
[2]Leadville and the Gold Belt, P. 48
[3]Leadville and the Gold Belt, P. 75-78.

Other gold producers were the Triumph, Lovejoy, Golden Chain Company, Miner Boy, Little Winnie, First National, Arena, Spot Cash, Antiock, Fannie Rawlings, Modoc, Garbutt, Midnight Valley, Nevada, Highland Chief, Lillian, Great Hopes, Nettie Morgan, Virginius, Australia, Colorado Prince, Louise, and Eliza.[1]

Leadville decided to celebrate her becoming one of the world's greatest gold producing camps, and so in the winter of 1895 invited the world to celebrate and feast with her. For this purpose a mammouth "Ice Palace" was erected, and a great "crystal carnival" arranged. Tingley S. Wood was chosen Director General and arranged the brilliant affair. Under his direction an army of workmen were set to work and a palace of ice arose on Capital Hill (just to the west of the city) the beauty of which can only be described by a poet. It covered 135,000 square feet, being 450 by 300 feet, contained ball rooms, beautifully decorated and brilliantly lighted. The structure was of the Norman Castellated style of architecture; the monotony of plain walls was relieved by beams and projecting buttresses, corbelling, and panelling. The main towers were of irregular pattern; those of the north front were octagonal. They were ninety feet high and forty feet in diameter. Their imposing height, reaching as they did above the walls and other towers, made them the most prominent object to meet the eye of the visitor. They were decorated by turrets on the eight corners of the

....

[1] Leadville and the Gold Belt, P. 81

octagon, and with panellings and battlements. The south towers were circular sixty feet high and thirty feet in diameter. The corner towers were also circular, being forty-five feet above ground and twenty feet in diameter.[1]

Within was a figure of "Leadville". This allegorical figure was nineteen feet in height and mounted on a twelve foot pedestal. Its outstretched arm pointed to the mineral hills, and carried a scroll with the camps production figures. There were also many other ice figures representing the home life of the people.[2]

The palace was majestic by day, but marvelous, dazzling by night when the myriads of lamps and great search lights flooded the structure. Skating, tobogganing, dancing, skiing, merry-go-rounds, etc., provided wonderful amusement for all. Davis writes "St. Paul, Quebec, Montreal, and Moscow have had their Ice Palaces and Carnivals, but Leadville never did things by halves, and it is claimed that for grandeur, size, expense and lavishness, Leadville surpassed them all".[3]

The new boom lasted until the great labor strike in June 1896. This unfortunate affair once more plunged the camp into deep depression, and virtually brought all work to a standstill. The history of the strike is a rather delicate subject to handle because of the bitterness of feeling aroused by that affair; also a rather difficult subject because of the cross fire of

....

1 C.C.Davis, P. 337-345.
2 C.C.Davis, P. 345-346.
3 C.C.Davis, P. 346-351

charges of conspiracy, attacks, murders, plots, etc. However, it seems the real history of it dates from 1893 when for reasons already described, there was a great falling off in the prices of silver and lead resulting in the closing of mines, and this in turn led to a great amount of unemployment. In order to eliminate this enforced idleness and to provide for a satisfactory wage and steady employment, a conference was held between the managers of the principal mines and representatives of the mines, as follows: P. W. Quilan, Thomas Cully, John Horgan, J.S. O'Brien, and John M. O'Neill. They arranged a schedule of wages and although it was below the average wage of the substantial period of 1880 to 1893, still it gave great satisfaction and provided steady employment in Leadville, when the rest of industrial America was still a victim of the panic.[1]

During the latter part of the year 1894, and still more so in 1895, Leadville enjoyed a great wave of prosperity, as already described, and because of this wave of prosperity, although the price of silver and lead declined still further, the miners felt justified in asking an increase of 50 cents per day for all $2.50 miners (price agreed on at conference of 1893), and also for all trammers, engineers, pumpmen, surface men, etc., unless they already were getting $3.00 a day.[2]

The mine managers did not feel able to meet this demand. Still a compromise might have been arranged, but suddenly on

....

[1]Judge Cavender and Reply of the Mine Managers, Dec. 10, 1896, P. 8 and 9.

[2]Judge Cavender; Also Mine Managers' Reply, P. 13.

Friday night, June 19, the leaders of the Miner's Union, many of them outsiders, called out all the $2.50 men. This immediately plunged the camp into a long, bitter, costly, and violent struggle. The conflicts, of every kind, from the hissing of mine managers by women and children to open battles between scabs and union men occurred. Most of the miners and laborers were good-natured law abiding American citizens, but there were some violent spirits among them and perhaps among their leaders, that suggested and carried out attacks which cast unjust reflections upon all the strikers.[1]

The struggle grew more intense and fights more frequent. The State Militia was brought in at the request of mine owners and city officials. The presence of the troops only made the struggle more bitter, until it culminated in the unfortunate attack on the Coronado and the Emmett.[2]

The Coronado mine, operated by the Coronado Mining Company of which E. T. Jeffrey was President, is located on East Seventh Street only about five blocks from Harrison Avenue. The manager of this property, R. B. Estey, decided early in September to attempt to reopen the mine with scab labor at the old wage of $2.50. The mine had been closed since June and as it was the first mine to attempt to reopen, aroused the wrath of many of the strikers. Most of the laborers, about 15 or 20 in number at the Coronado, slept and ate at the mine. The shaft house and engine

....

[1]Judge Cavender; Also Mine Managers' Reply, P. 18-19.
[2]Judge Cavender and Mine Managers' Reply, P. 19.

room were enclosed by a high board fence, and an interior stockade erected in preparation for the expected attack.[1]

During the night of Sunday, September 20, vague rumors were afloat that an attack was to be made. The men at the mine prepared for trouble. About one o'clock in the morning, the moon was hidden behind a heavy bank of clouds, but in the half light, bands of armed men could be seen silently appreaching the mine through the alley from the East. There were probably two hundred armed men around the mine, when suddenly there was a terrible explosion. A dynamite bomb had been thrown over the fence aimed at the big tank which contained several hundred gallons of fuel oil. Scarcely had the detonation died away before the rifles of the attacking party began to speak. The fusilade was terrific. A deadly fire was powered into the Coronado from the north, south, and east sides. Presently another bomb was hurled and this time a portion of the east fence was blown down, and another fellowed which blew off the top of the tank and the oil began to flow out in a small stream. Firebrands were also thrown in, and it was clear the attackers were making headway. The defenders, however, were also active. The fire continued for nearly an hour and it is estimated that not less than four thousand shots were fired. By this time the oil tank was blazing and the attackers turned their attention to keeping the citizens and fire department at bay. In the attempt by the fire department to lay a hose to the mine, Foreman Jerry O'Keefe was killed by one of the strikers and before

....

1 Mine Managers' Reply, P. 23.

the department, with the help of armed citizens, could secure control, the mine buildings and a number of dwelling houses in the neighborhood were destroyed.[1]

The Emmett mine had also resumed work a few days before, and as soon as the attack on the Coronado had been crowned with success, about two hundred and fifty armed men moved up there and lined up on a little slope just north of the fence. About 2:30 A.M., they promptly opened fire and threw several dynamite bombs, blowing down the fence. A rush was made through this opening, but was received with a heavy volley. The attackers fell back, taking their dead and wounded with them. They formed and charged again; this time aiding their move by discharging a cannon loaded with chain and shot, but the defenders were too well prepared, and succeeded in beating off the attack. There is no doubt that a large number were killed and wounded in this affair, and an attempt was made by the Grand Jury to secure convictions of some of those involved, but without success.[2]

The strike lasted so long and was so serious that the production from the Leadville Mines for 1896 was only a little better than half of what had been produced the previous year.[3]

This strike also retarded the development of the down town district.[4]

....

[1]Mine Managers' Reply, P. 23-24-25; Judge Cavender.
[2]Judge Cavender; Mine Managers' Reply, P. 26-27.
[3]See production figures given at end of this chapter.
[4]Elks Convention Pamphlet.

Other serious set-backs in this period, though of a much more temporary nature, were the big snow blockade of the early months of 1899 and the smelter strike later in the same year. This last strike did not cause severe or long disturbance.[1]

Much of the area famous during the gold days was abandoned after the labor strike of 1896, but in 1899 Major A.V.Bohn, one of the great mining leaders throughout this period, undertook the unwatering of the Penrose and other properties. Many mining men were skeptical, but the Home Mining Company kept up the work and was successful until the panic of 1907 caused the price of metals to drop.

Again the camp was depressed; a great many again left, once more convinced, as thousand of others had been at each previous period of depression, that the end of the producing days of the great camp had come. The combined production for 1908 and 1909 was less than of 1906 or even 1907.

Everything was almost at a complete standstill when the fickle goddess of chance once more waved her wand, and again Leadville became the world's greatest metal producer. This time it was a new ore. Leadville had long been familiar with Zinc in the form of sulphide, but this had never been profitable. In the early days it was a detriment in smelting; by 1900 there was a market for rich high-grade zinc sulphide, but the richer sulphides were soon worked out.

....

[1]Elks Convention Pamphlet.

Then in 1910 it was discovered by some casual tests that Zinc existed in a hitherto unsuspected form. Carbonate of Zinc, or smithsonite, and calamine, are well-known metals, but miners, geologists, and mineralogists had been working through immense deposits of these ores in the Leadville Mines without suspecting their existence in commercial quantities. They had long been piled on the dump as valueless, but now Fryer Hill, the home of the Little Pittsburgh, was once more aboom. The Hayden, already abandoned, became a great producer.[1]

On Carbonate Hill, the Western Mining Company, controlling the Maid of Erin, the Wolftone (one of the world's greatest zinc mines today) and other famous old producers, under the management of Samuel D. Nicholson, became a tremendous producer.[2]

Once more Leadville was the leading camp. Then in 1911 a new form of gold mining was launched. The Derry Ranch Gold Dredging Company placed an immense boat or dredge upon the old Derry place. This is the humblest of all forms of mining. Yet I saw it in operation when it was taking out $10,000 every two weeks, which is an average of $1.00 a minute, and still the ground shows no trace of yellow.

And one day I stood on the bank taking a picture of this great float, when an old miner approached, and after a moments conversation said, pointing up the gulch:"I was there when we took gold out with a pan; later we used the cradle and the Long Tom; than came Hydraulic mining and deep lode

....

1 and 2 C.C.Davis.

mining, and now this", and pointing over to where the dredge was piling up a huge mound of rock and gravel, he continued:

"I will not, but you will live to see the day when some one else with a new process comes along and takes gold out of those rocks they are throwing away now."

There are also tremendous pumping enterprises being carried on today. Perhaps the great pumps at the Penrose which are used to drain the mines above as well as the Penrose are of the greatest interest.

The production of this period is as follows:

1893	- - - -	$ 8,579,164.87
1894	- - - -	8,160,074.57
1895	- - - -	13,318,774.86
1896	- - - -	6,903,055.66
1897	- - - -	7,618,800.86
1898	- - - -	Estimated at 8,000,000.00
1899	- - - -	9,672,374.61
1900	- - - -	12,900,652,58
1901	- - - -	11,446,338.56
1902	- - - -	9,468,544.25
1903	- - - -	9,373,479.00
1904	- - - -	11,708,812.00
1905	- - - -	13,164,198.00
1906	- - - -	15,166,893.25[1]
1907	- - - -	12,626,139.51
1908	- - - -	6,692,139.52
1909	- - - -	6,844,186.48
1910	- - - -	7,034,450;94
1911	- - - -	8,227,016.67
1912	- - - -	11,182,616.17
1913	- - - -	9,040,358.68
1914	- - - -	9,087,627.58[2]

....

1 Banner year up to 1915

2 These figures are taken from the New Year Edition of the Leadville Herald Democrat, following each year mentioned.

CHAPTER VIII

THE MODERN LEADVILLE

In 1915, the Leadville produced $15,895,299.99 worth of precious metals. There were eight metals mined in this district: gold, lead, silver, iron, zinc, copper, manganese, and bismuth. The total production to date is nearly half a billion dollars.

Although Leadville is still a great mining center and has a great mining future, it is far different from the Rush Days. Today it is quiet, orderly, and well-governed. The mining is scientific and lacks the spectacularness of the old days. The town likewise is changed and strictly modern. Perhaps an editorial on "The Evolution of Leadville" from the Herald Democrat, modern Leadville's excellent, but only daily, will give the best picture of the present city. It is from the issue of January 1, 1916, and is as follows:

"If the men who came here in 1878, for the purpose of developing the infant industry of mining had realized fully the possibilities that were before them, and that another generation would follow in their footsteps, it is possible that they might have given more attention to the laying out of the city, and making the ground plans for permanency and stability. When the great surge of '79 came it found little on which to build, and everybody too busy to give adequate attention to municipal affairs as such. There was none of that colonizing instinct which is so essential in the building up of a new country. Consequently the place never took on the appearance of a new settlement, but rather of a hastily thrown together collection of buildings, some more pretentious than others, but still rather

more speculative than otherwise.

"Men who have since grown gray here came to Leadville to make a pile of money and leave. The idea that anyone would care to call this faraway country at the head of the Arkansas "home" seemed to be absurd. Most of the newcomers had left their people behind, and they could never reconcile it with the idea of home. Many of them could not become accustomed to the peculiar scenery of the Rockies, the bleak mountain tops making the long gray skyline, the snowy summits, and the barren unproductive soil.

"So Leadville had a bad beginning, and the opportunities which could have been utilized were passed by. Financial resources which were abundant were frittered away, and even worse conditions prevailed. There certainly was no need for the existence of the early day reign of extravagance and outright corruption, and there probably would have been much less of it, had there been any public sentiment at all, which concerned itself with the task of city building.

It must be admitted considering the amount of wealth that the district has produced that only an infinitesimal percentage of it has remained here in the shape of permanent improvements. This is a condition for which nobody can be held responsible, for the reason that there seemed to pervade the whole community the idea that this was but a temporary abiding place.

And yet with such an inauspicious beginning, Leadville has managed to build up a very respectable city, for finally a goodly proportion of the people discovered that they would probably remain. They found that they could live here as comfortably

and even as luxuriously as anywhere else, and as the seasons rolled by and it was realized that the climatic conditions were exceptionally delightful, free from unusual extremes of heat and cold, and peculiarly healthful and invigorating, the mountains became a center of attraction rather than desolate and repellant. Railroads have brought to our doors all that luxury and refinement may desire or a fastidious taste suggest. Over three decades of municipal existence have sandpapered away the early crudities, and have furnished the foundation for a municipality built up strong and vigorous out of the social and business life of the community.

"Schools, churches, lodges and clubs devoted to the work of civic betterment have all taken root and thrived here. There was a time when a "movement" looking to the permanent public good would have received scant attention, as the people were too busy making money to give a thought to these matters. But Leadville has been the focus and center of a "Good Roads" movement which has found expression in a most excellent system of highways. The advent of the automobile in Leadville is largely responsible for this, and the assurance that next season the number of automobilists will be greatly increased gives assurance that there will be a larger following than ever in the "Good Roads" movement.

"The Woman's Club has set an excellent example in the matter of Clean Up days, in suggestions for beautifying the home, in tree planting, and in protection to wild birds and flowers. All this has added to the local feeling, that after all, Leadville is a good place in which to live, and if a

man is only going to leave in order to find a corner in which to die, he might as well endeavor to render himself as comfortable and happy here as possible.

"There are few of the modern conveniences of civilization lacking here. Three hospitals, for instance, well equipped, modern, and served by staffs of surgeons and physicians as highly trained and skilled as can be found anywhere in the State, fill a particular need in a community like Leadville, where there is such a large percentage of single men, and where mine and smelter accidents are of such frequent occurrence.

"St. Luke's Hospital, St. Vincent's and the Lake County Hospital are three institutions of relief and mercy of which any city may be proud.

"Lodge life has enjoyed a remarkable development here, for the reason that men have felt the need of these voluntary associations for mutual aid, and for the social life accorded to be practically a necessity in a community where the sources and opportunities of amusement were limited. Fraternal and insurance societies enjoy a large membership, and other organizations of a more purely social character flourish here because they fill a part of the life of the individual which is so essential to his happiness. There may be the exceptional few who are all sufficient unto themselves, but there is a stronger tie in such fellowships as Masonry, Odd Fellowship, the Pythian Brotherhood, and the domain of the Elks, Moose, and Eagles, and such brotherhoods have proved of strong and lasting benefit. Many a man, left friendless and alone in the world, has found in this local lodge life, something which has made life for him worth while.

An organization which has come into existence in the past few years, for the purpose of promoting the welfare of the community, and acting as a central point about which movements for civic betterment, is the Leadville Commercial Club. Ever since Leadville awakened to the fact that some sort of civic organization was needed there have been attempts to get the business men together for mutual benefit. It has not been an easy task, as the failure of various organizations indicates. But in various ways each one served some good purpose, and in particular emphasized the need of constant cooperation.

The present Commercial Club was established a few years ago, and seems to have been founded on a firm basis. It has taken up movements, such as "Good Roads", has given encouragement to local enterprise and taken an interest in many minor details of local welfare. Its comfortable headquarters in the Hotel Vendome give an air of homelikeness to the organization, as it assures it a local habitation, and a definiteness and permanency that ensures stability.

BIBLIOGRAPHY

J.P.Whitney - Silver Mining Regions of Colorado. (New York, 1865)

Ovando J. Hollister - The Mines of Colorado. (Springfield, Mass., 1867)

Ned E. Farrell - Colorado. - (Chicago, 1868)

Frank Fossett - Colorado. - (Denver, 1876)
A Historical, Descriptive, and Statistical Work on The Rocky Mountain Gold and Silver Mining Region.

Frank Fossett - Colorado. - (New York, 1879)

Stephen F. Smart, - Colorado Miner, An 1879 Guide to Leadville. (Kansas Pacific R.R., Kansas City, Mo., 1879)

History of the Arkansas Valley, Colorado. (O. L. Bankin and Company, Chicago, 1881)

Alice Polk Hill -- Tales of the Colorado Pioneer. (Denver, 1884)

Frank Hall - History of the State of Colorado. Volume II. (Chicago, 1889)

Hubert Howe Bancroft - History of Nevada, Colorado, and Wyoming 1540-1888. (San Francisco, 1890) Volume XXV)

Manning, O'Keefe and DeLashmett - Leadville and the Gold Belt. (Leadville, 1895)

Lincoln H. Hall - Cripple Creek Up-To-Date. (Cripple Creek, 1896)

J. E. Snook - Colorado History and Government. (Denver, 1904)

F. L. Paxson - The County Boundaries of Colorado. (Boulder, Colorado, August 1906)
Reprinted from University of Colorado Studies, Volume III, No. 4.

Elks Convention Pamphlet of June 1907. (Leadville, 1907)

Eugene Parsons - The Making of Colorado. (Chicago, 1908)

Carlyle C. Davis - Memories. (San Francisco, 1915)

Newspapers

Leadville Chronicle

Carbonate Weekly Chronicle

Leadville Weekly Herald

Leadville Herald Democrat

Denver News

New York Graphic, 1881.

Documents

U.S.Geological Survey - Monographs, Vol. XII, by Samuel Franklin Emmons, entitled

"Geology and Mining Industry of Leadville, Colorado." (Washington, 1886)

Communication of Miners' Union to Governor McIntyre and People of Colorado. (November 25, 1896)

Reply to this by Mine Managers - (December 10, 1896)

Files of the Pioneer Society

Market Quotations for Metals

Production Records, etc.

Individuals

A.Y.Corman came to Leadville in May 1860.

C. W. Derry came to Leadville in 1862.

P. G. Noris came to Leadville in 1870.

"Con" Cunningham came to Leadville in 1874.

C. Hearsey came to Leadville in 1876.

Mrs. Thomas Starr came to Leadville in 1876.

N. J. Arnold came to Leadville in 1878.

Judge Charles Cavender came to Leadville in 1878.

Ex.-Lieutenant-Governor Peter W. Breene came to Leadville in 1878.

James R. McNeece came to Leadville in 1878.

William Thompson came to Leadville in 1879.

George Broughton came to Leadville in 1879.

C. J. Deane came to Leadville in 1879.

"Mc." McGage came to Leadville in 1879.

Judge McLoud came to Leadville in 1879.

E. B. Harlan came to Leadville in 1879.

Captain Jenks came to Leadville in 1879.

C. H. S. Whipple came to Leadville in 1879.

James Robinson came to Leadville in 1879.

James M. Knight came to Leadville in 1881.

A. G. Verhofstad came to Leadville in 1881.

In addition many individuals who came at a later date were of value in helping to check various items, also for details of events during the more recent periods.

Hollister, Emmons, and Fossett were of value upon the "Placer" and "Discovery of the Carbonate" periods. The History of the Arkansas Valley and C.C.Davis were of great assistance on the Rush Periods, and Leadville and the Gold Belt upon the early nineties.

However, the most valuable material of all was received from individuals who were eye-witnesses of the events of the period for which they were used. These men varied greatly in

knowledge, accuracy, and the value of their evidence. On the whole, I found them reliable only for the first year or two of their experience in camp. In this way I was able to check the various stories. There was always a tendency to go to extremes, and to exaggerate. I was usually on the guard for this and only occasionally got the "fever" myself.

The newspapers were of value in checking dates, names, details, etc. of events later than 1878.

CPSIA information can be obtained at www.ICGtesting.com
Printed in the USA
LVOW05s0925161113

361578LV00004B/312/P